CHEVY
CLASSICS

CHEVY
CLASSICS

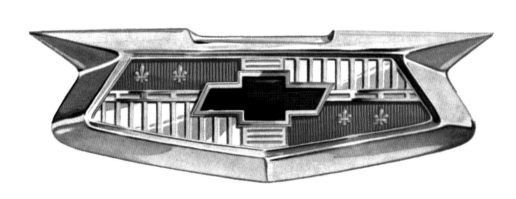

BY THE AUTO EDITORS OF CONSUMER GUIDE®

Publications International, Ltd.

Handwritten inscription: to Max, Keep a smile on your face and your eyes on the road! cheers, Prof J. 12-16-19

Louis Weber, CEO
Publications International, Ltd.
7373 North Cicero Avenue
Lincolnwood, Illinois 60712

Permission is never granted for commercial purposes.

ISBN-13: 978-1-4127-1524-9
ISBN-10: 1-4127-1524-5

Manufactured in China.

8 7 6 5 4 3 2 1

Library of Congress Control Number: 2007933666

Credits

Photography:

The editors would like to thank the following people and organizations for supplying the photography that made this book possible. They are listed below, along with the page number(s) of their photos.

Thomas Glatch: 55, 73, 123; **Jerry Heasley:** 71, 83, 89; **John Heilig:** 93; **Don Heiny:** 53; **Jeff Johnson:** 21; **Nick Komic:** 81; **Vince Manocchi:** 9, 19, 27, 29, 33, 47, 49, 77, 87, 91, 109; **Roger Mattingly:** 25; **Doug Mitchel:** 23, 31, 45, 57, 59, 61, 85, 95, 97, 103, 107, 111; **Ron Moorhead:** 101; **Mike Mueller:** 35, 43; **Robert Nicholson:** 75, 99, 115; **Nina Padgett:** 121; **Mark Sincavage:** 13; **Tom Storm:** 127; **David Temple:** 69; **W. C. Waymack:** 37, 41, 51, 63, 65, 79, 105, 113, 117, 119, 125; **Nicky Wright:** 11, 15, 39, 67

Back Cover: Vince Manocchi; Doug Mitchel

Owners:

Special thanks to the owners of the cars featured in this book for their cooperation. Their names and the page number(s) for their vehicles follow.

Mike Allen: 117; **David Anderson:** 67; **Norman Andrews:** 97; **Bill Bush:** 91; **Joe Carfagna:** 53; **Lew Clark:** 11; **Marilyn Cliff:** 105; **Corvette Mike:** 107; **Tony D'Amico:** 103; **Greg Englin:** 57; **John Finster:** 77; **Bob Flack:** 39; **Theodore Freeman:** 35; **Tom and Christine French:** 119; **Larry Gordon:** 59, back cover; **Bill Gratchic:** 127; **Peter Guido, Jr.:** 17; **Chuck Henderson:** 61; **Bill Hoff:** 89; **Tony Hossain:** 81; **Joe James:** 63; **John and Barbara James:** 121; **Roger James:** 21; **Cory King:** 115; **Tom Korbas:** 85; **Herb Krombach:** 13; **Edward Kuziel:** 43; **Bob Macy:** 71, 83; **Jack Macy:** 15; **Larry Martin:** 41; **Jack and Jan Matske:** 45; **Mike and Kay Maxson:** 69; **Tom Meleo:** 9, back cover; **Gary Mills:** 49; **Connie and Larry Mitchell:** 75, 99; **John Murray:** 29, back cover; **Dennis Pagliano:** 47, back cover; **Sam Pierce:** 73; **Norman Plogge:** 31; **John Poochigian:** 19; **Robert Richards:** 23; **Robert Rocchio:** 27; **Jim and Chris Ross:** 109; **Andy and Merlene Rueve:** 65; **Kim and Judy Ryan:** 113; **Rod Ryan:** 55; **Ed Stackman:** 123; **Kimberly Strauss:** 93; **Jim and Chery Utrecht:** 79; **Howard and Yvonne Van Der Eb:** 87; **Volo Auto Museum:** 111; **Donald Walkemeyer:** 37; **Leo Welter:** 101; **Rosalie and Jim Wente:** 51; **Karl Wilke:** 25; **Leroy and Judy Williams:** 125; **Mike and Laurie Yager:** 95

contents

foreword

The Chevrolet story is an American story. It's a tale of an underdog on the outside looking in and dreaming big. It's a story of persistently working away at a goal, and then succeeding, perhaps beyond anybody's expectations.

Chevrolet was founded by an unlikely underdog—William C. Durant. He loved the art of the deal and put together General Motors in 1908, overreached with acquisitions, and was forced out of the company by 1910. Unbowed, he quickly bounced back to form the Chevrolet Motor Car Company the following year, naming it after former Buick factory-team racer Louis Chevrolet.

The first Chevrolet car was a large 6-cylinder tourer, but Durant had his sights set on the appealing, but formidable, target

that was the wildly popular Ford Model T. Durant wanted to sell a lot of small, inexpensive cars, which he did—enough, in fact, to use the profits to buy back GM in 1915.

By 1920, Durant was out again, but Chevrolet had become part of the GM family. An assessment of the corporation's confused product roster in the early '20s recommended discontinuing the marque. What a mistake that would have been! In 1927, it surpassed Ford in sales for the first time and was about to start an incredible streak as "USA-1" that would span decades.

This success relied on cars that struck a chord with Americans, meeting their needs for style, economy, and performance. Herein are some of the great ones from Chevy's greatest days.

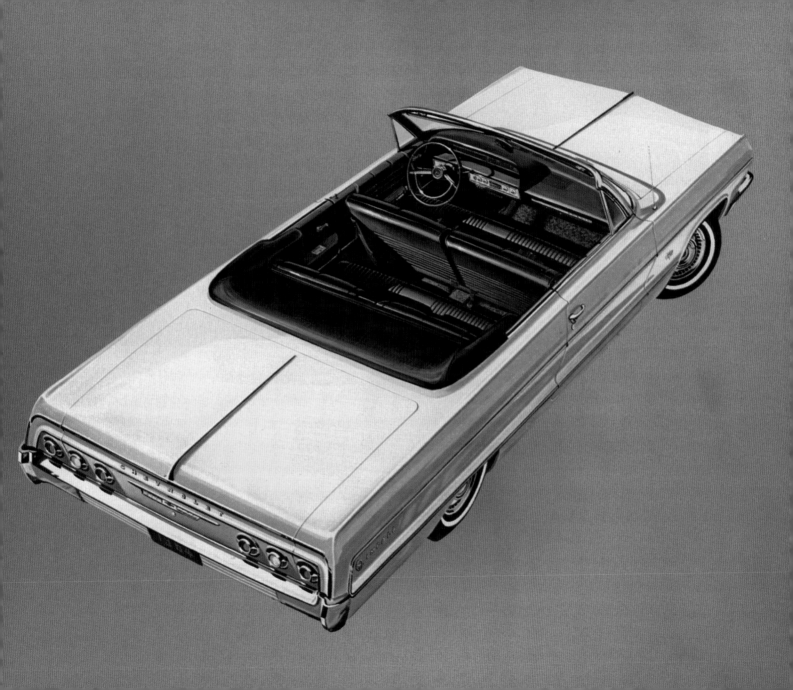

For Economical Transportation
CHEVROLET
"Four-Ninety"
ROADSTER

CHEVROLET

1920
490

The first car to bear the Chevrolet name, the Classic Six, brought to the surface the differing visions of the make's founder, William C. Durant, and its designer/namesake, Louis Chevrolet. In short order, Louis and his large, expensive 6-cylinder cars were out and Billy's small, cheap 4-cylinder machines were in. To Durant, the target was the Ford Model T. For 1916, he brought out the 490, so named for its introductory price—which then just happened to match the tab for Henry Ford's "Tin Lizzie." Offered until 1922, the 102-inch-wheelbase 490 was powered by a 20-hp engine of 171 cid. The 1920 models had new reverse-curve front fenders. The tourer (opposite) was one of four available body styles. Its $810 price was cut to $735 by the end of the year.

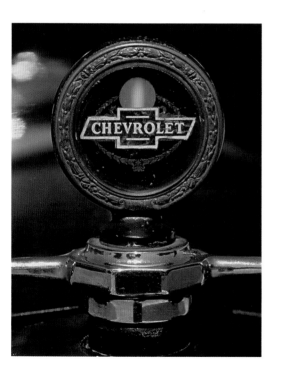

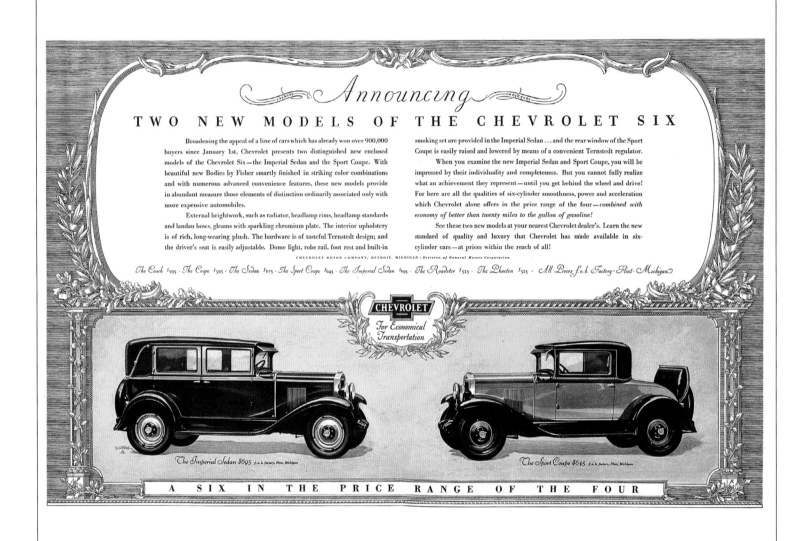

Announcing
TWO NEW MODELS OF THE CHEVROLET SIX

Broadening the appeal of a line of cars which has already won over 900,000 buyers since January 1st, Chevrolet presents two distinguished new enclosed models of the Chevrolet Six—the Imperial Sedan and the Sport Coupe. With beautiful new Bodies by Fisher smartly finished in striking color combinations and with numerous advanced convenience features, these new models provide in abundant measure those elements of distinction ordinarily associated only with more expensive automobiles.

External brightwork, such as radiator, headlamp rims, headlamp standards and landau bows, gleams with sparkling chromium plate. The interior upholstery is of rich, long-wearing plush. The hardware is of tasteful Ternstedt design; and the driver's seat is easily adjustable. Dome light, robe rail, foot rest and built-in

smoking set are provided in the Imperial Sedan . . . and the rear window of the Sport Coupe is easily raised and lowered by means of a convenient Ternstedt regulator.

When you examine the new Imperial Sedan and Sport Coupe, you will be impressed by their individuality and completeness. But you cannot fully realize what an achievement they represent—until you get behind the wheel and drive! For here are all the qualities of six-cylinder smoothness, power and acceleration which Chevrolet alone offers in the price range of the four—*combined with economy of better than twenty miles to the gallon of gasoline!*

See these two new models at your nearest Chevrolet dealer's. Learn the new standard of quality and luxury that Chevrolet has made available in six-cylinder cars—at prices within the reach of all!

CHEVROLET MOTOR COMPANY, DETROIT, MICHIGAN · *Division of General Motors Corporation*

The Coach $595 · The Coupe $595 · The Sedan $675 · The Sport Coupe $645 · The Imperial Sedan $695 · The Roadster $525 · The Phaeton $525 · All Prices f.o.b. Factory · Flint · Michigan

CHEVROLET
For Economical Transportation

The Imperial Sedan $695 f.o.b. factory, Flint, Michigan

The Sport Coupe $645 f.o.b. factory, Flint, Michigan

A SIX IN THE PRICE RANGE OF THE FOUR

1929
AC International

Beginning in 1931, Chevrolet would enjoy a rarely interrupted reign of more than 50 years as "USA-1" in sales. For most of the first half of that stretch, Chevy's success rested on cars powered solely by simple, economical 6-cylinder engines that could trace their lineage to the powerplant introduced for 1929. Though not the first 6 in the make's history, the "stovebolt"—so named because of its slotted head bolts—was its first with overhead valves. Cast-iron pistons helped keep a lid on production costs. The 194-cid engine made 46 hp at 2600 rpm. Chevrolet added some new models to the 107-inch-wheelbase AC International series during the '29 selling season. Among them was the sport coupe (right) with a rumble seat. It cost $645—$50 more than a two-passenger coupe.

DISCRIMINATING PEOPLE HAVE MADE THIS CAR THE VOGUE

It is a noteworthy fact that those fortunate people with good taste, and the means to gratify it, have singled out the new Chevrolet Six for their approval. The reasons are not difficult to find, for the new Chevrolet has everything they naturally insist upon in a personal car. Its Fisher bodies are so smartly styled and finished that they show to advantage even alongside expensive custom cars. Interiors have the charm that only fine, beautifully tailored upholsteries and modishly designed fittings can confer. Lounge-type seats, finger-touch adjustable driver's seat, quick, silent Syncro-Mesh gear-shifting combined with Free Wheeling, and easily-worked controls assure restful comfort and relaxation while driving. And the fast, smooth, and quiet six-cylinder engine brings you to the end of the longest journey without a hint of nervous fatigue. In fact, the more you think about it, the more logical it is that the new Chevrolet Six should become the vogue in smart personal transportation.

• • •

Twenty distinctive models priced as low as $475, f. o. b. Flint, Michigan. Special equipment extra. Low delivered prices and easy G. M. A. C. terms. Chevrolet Motor Co., Detroit, Michigan. Division of General Motors.

NEW
CHEVROLET
SIX

THE GREAT AMERICAN VALUE

1932

BA Confederate

Throughout his long career as General Motors' chief of styling, Harley Earl often sought to bring some uppercrust Cadillac looks to workaday Chevrolets. He succeeded spectacularly in that pursuit for 1932. Graceful radiator, hood, and fender shapes were scaled-down versions of Cadillac elements. The dual horns and chrome hood-vent doors found on DeLuxe models also recalled details found on period Caddys. Frankly, in the depths of the Great Depression, with sales down drastically throughout the industry, Chevy really needed the style boost to stay atop the sales charts. Rival Ford had stolen the headlines with its new V-8 engine. Meanwhile, the Chevrolet 6 got a 10-hp hike (to 60). Also new was an easier-shifting Synchromesh three-speed transmission.

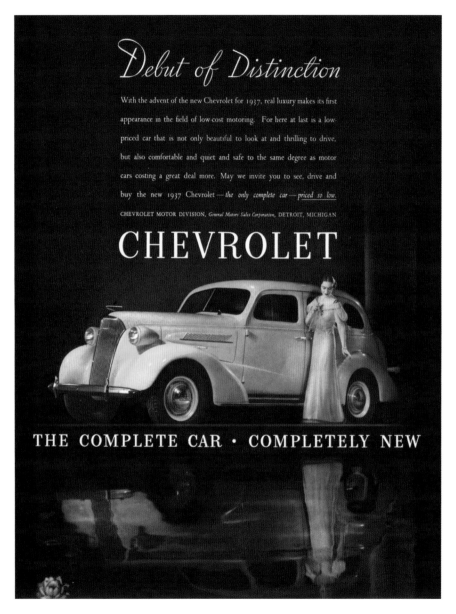

1937
Master

The 1937 Chevrolet was completely new, from its roomier all-steel Fisher bodies with "diamond crown speedline" styling to the 112.3-inch wheelbase. Perhaps most notable, however, was its second-generation "stovebolt" 6. Revised bore and stroke dimensions, a stronger crankshaft, domed pistons, the addition of a fourth main bearing, and a quarter-point compression boost were all part of the recipe. At 85 hp, the 216.5-cid engine matched the advertised horsepower of the Ford V-8. Top-line Master DeLuxes featured "Knee Action" independent front suspension, which was revised for '37. For about $70 less, buyers could have a Master with a beam front axle. At $619, the two-seat Master business coupe (opposite) was the year's cheapest Chevy.

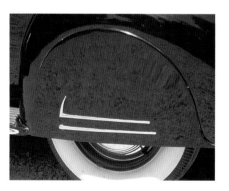

Today's Performance-Leader!

First in Acceleration··First in Hill-Climbing

...and First in Sales too!

It's the **LIVELIEST** of all low-priced cars!

Lucky the man, or the lady, who owns a new 1939 Chevrolet!

They are driving today's performance-leader—*the liveliest of all low-priced cars*—with a mighty supply of quick, eager, reserve power packed into its famous valve-in-head engine.

When traffic has started moving, and every driver steps on the accelerator with the thought of "going places," *it's the Chevrolet driver who safely takes the lead!*

And when the scene changes to open country, and high hills loom ahead, *it's the Chevrolet driver again who goes over the top with the greatest of ease!*

First in acceleration! First in hill-climbing! First in all-round efficiency with economy! That's the story of this fleet, safe motor car, and, incidentally, *that is why it is first in sales among all cars in the nation!*

Drive the winner! Place your order now for a new Chevrolet!

CHEVROLET MOTOR DIVISION, *General Motors Sales Corporation*, DETROIT, MICHIGAN
General Motors Installment Plan—convenient, economical monthly payments

No other car combines all these famous features:

EXCLUSIVE VACUUM GEARSHIFT

NEW AERO-STREAM STYLING, NEW BODIES BY FISHER

NEW LONGER RIDING-BASE

85-HORSEPOWER VALVE-IN-HEAD SIX

PERFECTED HYDRAULIC BRAKES

NEW "OBSERVATION CAR" VISIBILITY

PERFECTED KNEE-ACTION RIDING SYSTEM with Improved Shockproof Steering *(Available on Master De Luxe models only)*

TIPTOE-MATIC CLUTCH

A GENERAL   MOTORS VALUE

CHEVROLET
The **only** low-priced car combining "ALL THAT'S **BEST** AT LOWEST COST!"

1939
Master DeLuxe

Nineteen thirty-nine was a year of some "firsts" and "lasts" in Chevrolet showrooms. The year marked the last go-round for the 1937-vintage bodies. It also saw the final stand for "flatback" sedans. New features included the optional availability of a vacuum-assisted gearshift lever mounted on the steering column and the adoption of coil-and-wishbone independent front suspension for Master DeLuxes. New frontal styling, again with Cadillac-inspired overtones, helped hide the fact that the bodies were in their third season. The built-in trunks of two-door town sedans and four-door sport sedans appeared more integrated than before—and finally rendered trunkless models obsolete. All in all, Chevrolet sales rebounded nicely from the dip experienced in recession-plagued 1938.

1941
Special DeLuxe

A beautiful new car with Buick-inspired looks greeted visitors to Chevrolet dealerships in 1941. A broad grille of horizontal bars sat between headlamps now fully integrated into the fenders. As bodies widened to provide three additional inches of interior hip room, running boards were concealed under lower-body sheetmetal. Also, a stylish Fleetline notchback 4-door sedan was added to the line. A new era was at hand. The beam axle was discontinued after 1940, so all Chevys now featured independent front suspension. Wheelbase stretched to 116 inches, and horsepower was raised to 90. The Special DeLuxe was the top series. Among its seven model offerings was the convertible coupe (opposite). Its $949 base price included a vacuum-operated top; 15,296 were made.

1942
Aerosedan

The world war that Americans had been warily eyeing from a distance finally engulfed them when Japanese forces attacked the U.S. Pacific Fleet at anchor in Hawaii on December 7, 1941. Less than two months later, the production of passenger cars came to a halt, their places on assembly lines taken by machines of war. Even before the last 1942 cars were made, they struck a martial note. To save limited chromium reserves, all cars manufactured after January 1 wore painted trim—and brightwork on finished cars not yet shipped had to be painted over. These were so-called "blackout" models. GM's trendy fastback "torpedo" body style was extended to Chevrolet in '42 as the Fleetline Aerosedan. An instant hit, the $880 car was the year's most popular Chevy with 61,855 made.

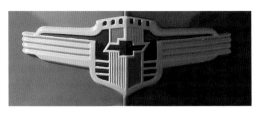

The Styleline De Luxe 4-Door Sedan.
White sidewall tires optional at extra cost.

The most Beautiful **BUY** *for Value*

... because only Chevrolet gives so **many** quality features at such low prices!

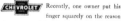 Recently, one owner put his finger squarely on the reason why more people buy Chevrolets than any other make of car, by saying—

"Measure motor cars by *quality*, or measure them by the *dollar sign*, and you'll find Chevrolet is *the most beautiful buy of all*."

And, indeed, where else will you find an automobile that offers so *many* advantages of highest-priced cars for so *little* money, considering purchase price, operation and upkeep!

Where else will you find a car that provides the enviable beauty of Body by Fisher . . . the totally new standard of driving and riding ease of Center-Point Design . . . and the pace-setting efficiency of a Valve-in-Head engine plus the greater motoring protection of safety plate glass throughout—all at the lowest prices!

All comparisons prove, *nowhere else do you get such high quality at such low cost* as in Chevrolet—the most beautiful buy for value—and America's first choice, again this year!

CHEVROLET MOTOR DIVISION, *General Motors Corporation*, DETROIT 2, MICHIGAN

FIRST FOR QUALITY
AT LOWEST COST

CHEVROLET

AMERICA'S CHOICE
FOR 18 YEARS

1949
Fleetline DeLuxe

When postwar auto production resumed for 1946, manufacturers first issued touched-up versions of their 1942 cars. Little by little, though, fresh designs started coming out. In 1949, it was Chevrolet's turn to join the parade. The '49s, with their lowered hoods and straight-through fenderlines, came in two trim levels: stark Special and nicer DeLuxe. All notchback styles and the station wagon—Chevy's last with structural-wood construction—were dubbed Stylelines. Fastback sedans, which included a new 4-door version (opposite), carried on the Fleetline name. Underneath, wheelbase was reined in slightly to 115 inches. "Center-Point Steering" and a lower center of gravity improved handling. A crisply operating new shifter mechanism replaced the slow vacuum device.

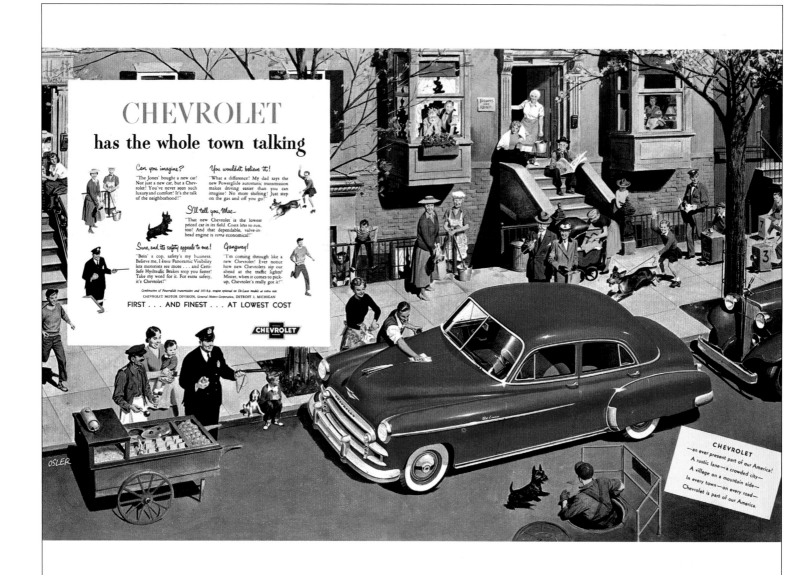

1950
DeLuxe Bel Air

The year after a full redesign usually meant a car with few changes. Trim might be altered. Perhaps a technical upgrade or two was made. Chevrolet did—and *didn't*—follow that script in 1950. Some teeth were deleted from the grille. A revised badge graced the hood and a new-style handle opened the trunk. The 6-cylinder engine gained two horsepower. Still, the year did see an all-new body style, the Bel Air hard-top coupe, and the first automatic transmission in the low-price field, the two-speed Power-glide. Following the lead set by Buick, Cadillac, and Oldsmobile in '49, the Bel Air delivered the look of a top-up convertible, albeit with closed-car comfort. To compensate for slippage during shifts, Powerglide-equipped cars came with a 105-hp 235.5-cid engine with hydraulic lifters.

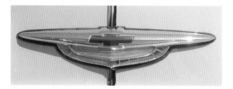

"See the U.S.A. in your Chevrolet..."

Only a few people have succeeded in making the rough trip down the rapids of this river ... but *millions* of men and women enjoy the gliding ride of Chevrolet's unitized Knee-Action. Recognize the river? It's the Colorado.

The Chevrolet Styleline De Luxe 4-Door Sedan (Continuation of standard equipment and trim illustrated is dependent on availability of material.)

Chevrolet's big curved windshield and Panoramic Visibility—large glass area all around—let you enjoy fully the scenic grandeur of "The Father of Waters" as you drive along the Mississippi Valley.

Roll along these majestic rivers
in the largest and finest of low-priced cars!

Great salmon fishing country, this. And if you travel there in a Chevrolet with Power-glide automatic transmission*—so smooth, so easy, so far ahead of the field—you'll be well rested and more than ready to wet a line in the beautiful Columbia River.

From the Hudson River Palisades, the crowds saw the first steamship on her maiden voyage. Speaking of "firsts," Chevrolet is nearly 40 years ahead of other low-priced cars in the development of the Valve-in-Head engine.

... and now you're on the open highway cruising along in the solid and satisfying comfort that Chevrolet *bigness* brings and Chevrolet *fineness* enhances.

For this is the *largest* and *finest* of low-priced cars!

It's longest and heaviest, with widest tread, for road-hugging, road-smoothing luxury.
It's finest in fine-car engineering features that add zest to your driving enjoyment.

Largest. Finest. And what you'll like best—
the Chevrolet line lists for less than the rest!

See your dealer. Chevrolet Division of General Motors, Detroit 2, Michigan.

Do you recognize this river, immortalized by Stephen Foster in one of the greatest songs of the South? It's the Swannee. Year after year, more people recognize the extra value that Chevrolet offers—and buy more Chevrolets than any other car.

CHEVROLET

POWER *Glide*
Automatic Transmission
No-Shift driving at its low-priced best combined with 105-h.p. Engine optional on De Luxe models at extra cost.

MORE PEOPLE BUY CHEVROLETS THAN ANY OTHER CAR!

HOLIDAY/OCTOBER

1951
Styleline DeLuxe

At first glance, it might seem that the newest thing about the 1951 model was its advertising slogan—"See the USA in your Chevrolet"—seen in print and heard on television (the latter in song from Dinah Shore). That, however, would be selling the '51s short. Rear fenders were raised and squared off and taillights were moved to their trailing edges. The grille featured newly pointed parking lights at the corners, and side trim was all new. Drivers faced a redesigned instrument panel and when they stepped on the brake pedal, larger binders stopped the car in a shorter span. A record 1.52 million Chevys were made for the 1950 model year, but output of the '51s slipped to 1.25 million. The $2030 DeLuxe convertible (opposite) accounted for 20,172 of them.

A long drive in this smart Sport Coupe leaves you rested, relaxed and ready for fun.

Pleasure?... Full measure!
Price?... Pleasant surprise!

If you think that high quality in a motor car goes hand in hand with high cost, your Chevrolet dealer has a very pleasant surprise for you.

You'll be surprised at the style and quality of Chevrolet's Body by Fisher ... the *only* Body by Fisher in the low-price field.

You'll be surprised at the smoothness of new Centerpoise Power ... with Chevrolet's famous valve-in-head engine centered, poised and cushioned in rubber by new high-side mountings.

You'll be surprised at the comfort of Chevrolet's improved Knee-Action ride ... at the easy way this car handles and its solid feel on the road.

In *every* respect, this fine, big Chevrolet offers you a full measure of motoring pleasure. And yet—most pleasant surprise of all—it's the lowest-priced line in its field! See your Chevrolet dealer soon and satisfy yourself that there's no reason for paying more. Chevrolet Division of General Motors, Detroit 2, Michigan.

MORE PEOPLE BUY CHEVROLETS THAN ANY OTHER CAR!

The Only Fine Cars **PRICED SO LOW!**

CHEVROLET

Smooth as a fine tennis court—that's Powerglide automatic transmission with extra-powerful Valve-in-Head engine and Automatic Choke. Optional on De Luxe models at extra cost.

Colorful as the most scenic course. Chevrolet offers a choice of 26 solid colors and two-tone color combinations with color-matched interiors in De Luxe models.

Room for two foursomes in this handsome Chevrolet Station Wagon with all-steel Body by Fisher. Four doors for easier entrance and exit.

Continuation of standard equipment and trim illustrated is dependent on availability of material.

1952
Styleline DeLuxe

Chevrolet model-year assemblies slumped to 818,142 cars, but that had as much to do with government-imposed production quotas related to the Korean War as it did with anything put out by the competition. Since materials were allocated to automakers in proportion to their 1951 sales performance, Chevy was guaranteed to hold its lead in '52. Cosmetic changes were confined to the grille—which grew five "teeth"—and side trim. Not only were there fewer Chevrolets made, there were also fewer of them from which to choose. The Styleline coupes, sedans, station wagon, convertible, and Bel Air hardtop (opposite) all were continued, but dwindling interest in fastbacks left just one Fleetline in the catalog, a two-door DeLuxe. It, too, would be gone after 1952.

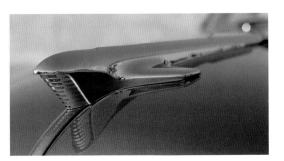

The Brilliant New "Two-Ten" 4-Door Sedan.

Expect these wonderful things from Chevrolet's new high-compression power . . .

No matter *where* or *how* you drive, Chevrolet's new high-compression power brings you many wonderful advantages.

You probably expect greater acceleration. And it's yours. You enjoy faster getaway and increased passing ability.

You, no doubt, count on climbing hills with new ease. And you do.

You can be sure of finer and more responsive performance under every driving condition. But with all this, you might *not* expect greater gasoline mileage. Yet you get it.

One reason is the new 115-h.p. "Blue-Flame" engine. Teamed with the new Powerglide* automatic transmission, this new valve-

in-head engine delivers more power than any other engine in the low-price field.

Another reason — the greatly advanced, 108-h.p. "Thrift-King" engine. This highly improved valve-in-head engine brings the same advantages of more power and higher compression to gearshift models.

Your Chevrolet dealer will be more than happy to demonstrate *all* the wonderful things you will find in America's most popular car. . . . Chevrolet Division of General Motors, Detroit 2, Michigan.

Combination of Powerglide automatic transmission and 115-h.p. "Blue-Flame" engine optional on "Two-Ten" and Bel Air models at extra cost. (Continuation of standard equipment and trim illustrated is dependent on availability of material.)

MORE PEOPLE BUY CHEVROLETS THAN ANY OTHER CAR!

1953
Two-Ten

Chevrolet went a bit "uptown" in 1953, applying the Bel Air name to a flashy new premium four-car series. The former DeLuxe became a mid-range line called the Two-Ten, and the budget Special became the One-Fifty. With its wide array of available body styles and prices mostly unchanged from 1952, the Two-Ten series was the volume seller of the Chevrolet family. Ironically, it played host to the year's rarest single model, a $2093 convertible that generated just 5617 orders. More than four times as many buyers opted for the Bel Air ragtop that cost only $82 more. Heavily facelifted bodies adopted a one-piece windshield. A 108-hp 235.5-cid 6 was the new base engine; cars with Powerglide (newly redone to permit low-gear starts) got a horsepower boost to 115.

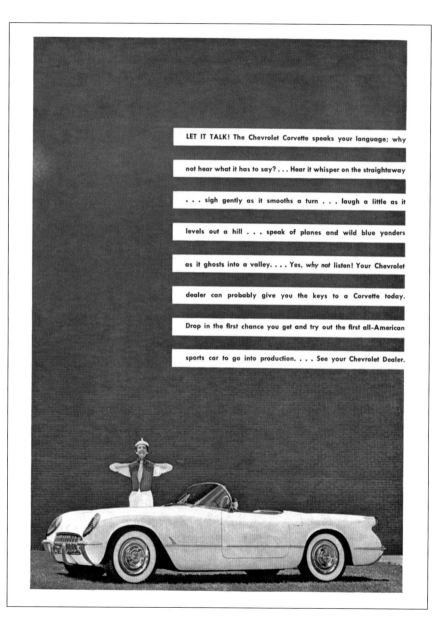

LET IT TALK! The Chevrolet Corvette speaks your language; why not hear what it has to say? . . . Hear it whisper on the straightaway . . . sigh gently as it smooths a turn . . . laugh a little as it levels out a hill . . . speak of planes and wild blue yonders as it ghosts into a valley. . . . Yes, *why not* listen! Your Chevrolet dealer can probably give you the keys to a Corvette today. Drop in the first chance you get and try out the first all-American sports car to go into production. . . . See your Chevrolet Dealer.

1954
Corvette

An American motoring legend was born in summer 1953 when Chevrolet began producing the Corvette. Just months before, the two-seat sports car had been a Harley Earl "dream car" in GM's traveling Motorama show. Given its late start and $3250 price tag, it's little wonder that a scant 300 were built that first year. With more vigorous promotion (including the first magazine advertising) and a choice of colors other than Polo White in 1954, demand rose to 3640. The Corvette's chief novelty was its lightweight fiberglass body. It was mounted on a 102-inch-wheelbase chassis with Chevy's first use of an open driveshaft. A triple-carbureted, dual-exhaust version of the 235-cid 6 hooked to the Powerglide transmission made 150 hp at first but was tweaked to 155 hp during 1954.

The new 1954 Chevrolet Bel Air Sport Coupe. With three great series, Chevrolet offers the most beautiful choice of models in its field.

How the new Chevrolet wrings more <u>power</u> and more <u>miles</u> out of every gallon of gas...

You see a couple of things in our picture up there that combine to make mighty fine motoring—the New England countryside and the new 1954 Chevrolet.

But *wherever* you live or drive, that new Chevrolet performance will please you in a number of special ways.

THERE HAS NEVER BEEN a Chevrolet that responded so quickly, smoothly and quietly to your foot on the accelerator. You accelerate, climb hills and whisper along the highway as you never did before.

NEW HIGH-COMPRESSION POWER is the reason behind these important advantages. Chevrolet has the *highest* compression ratio in any leading low-priced car. And high-compression is the key to another very pleasing and very important fact about Chevrolet performance.

IT'S A LONG WAY FROM "FULL" TO "EMPTY." Higher compression means that the fuel mixture is squeezed more tightly in the engine to get more work out of the same amount of gas. That is how Chevrolet gives you more power and finer performance with important gas savings. That is why the Chevrolet gas gauge takes such a long time and so many miles to move from "full" to "empty."

FINE, ECONOMICAL PERFORMANCE over the miles is only one reason why you'll *always* be glad you bought a Chevrolet. No other low-priced car offers you so many important advantages including all the automatic features and power controls you could want. Yet, *Chevrolet is the lowest-priced line of cars.*

See Your Chevrolet Dealer

MORE PEOPLE BUY CHEVROLETS THAN ANY OTHER CAR!

POWERGLIDE NOW AVAILABLE ON ALL MODELS! Now you can enjoy Powerglide—the *zippy, thrifty* automatic transmission—on all models in all three series. And Powerglide has proved its ruggedness and dependability over more owner-driven miles than any other automatic transmission in Chevrolet's field. Teamed with the "Blue-Flame 125" engine, Powerglide is optional at extra cost.

SYMBOL OF SAVINGS
CHEVROLET
EMBLEM OF EXCELLENCE

1954
Bel Air

Detail changes—grille, taillights, and front bumper chief among them—differentiated 1954 Chevrolet family cars from their immediate forebears. Horsepower was up to as much as 125, and more power accessories joined the options list. Still, starting prices rose by just $10. That's not what made them stand out, though. The '54s would be the last strictly 6-cylinder, torque-tube-drive, "economy-before-thrills" Chevys. A complete revolution in styling and engineering was in the wings, and it would totally recast the marque's image. As they had in '53, high-end Bel Airs featured standard fender skirts and a daggerlike dash of contrast paint on the rear fenders. Hardtops sported two-tone cloth-and-vinyl upholstery and an eight-passenger station wagon joined the series.

THE NEW CHEVROLET DELRAY *features club coupe styling, sedan roominess, and a washable all-vinyl interior that's made for family wear.*

Dressed for chores—or children

A CHEVROLET DELRAY doesn't mind dusty overalls . . . or the children's feet . . . or a few boxes of tomatoes piled onto the back seat. Its handsome, hardy all-vinyl interior wears like saddle leather . . . and rides about seventeen times softer. It's easy as soapsuds to keep it looking new. This is one car you can take soap and water to *inside*.

Like other Motoramic Chevrolet models, the Delray has that nice uncluttered look about its styling. Sweet and simple, and as clean as sunlight. Tie that to one of the new engines (either a six, or the 162-horsepower V8 or the 180-horse-power V8) and you've got a car to be proud of. Many of the things you'll especially like about your Chevrolet—out-rigger rear springs, Anti-Dive braking, a big 12-volt electrical system—are features that a lot of other cars wish they had. Your Chevrolet dealer's the man to see. . . . Chevrolet Division of General Motors, Detroit 2, Michigan.

motoramic Chevrolet
Stealing the thunder from the high-priced cars!

1955
Two-Ten Delray

Between the spirit provided by a new ohv V8 engine and the sparkle from fresh styling, Chevrolet turned out a line of 1955 models destined to be sales leaders in their day and enthusiast icons ever since. Chief engineer Ed Cole went to work on the V8 as soon as he arrived at Chevy in 1952. The result was a 265-cid "Turbo Fire" mill that made 162 hp in base form, or 180 with a four-barrel carburetor and dual exhausts. Meanwhile, stylists led by Clare MacKichan turned out a low, contemporary beauty. The midlevel Two-Ten continued to garner the most sales. Among its six available models was the Delray. Advertised as a club coupe, it shared its body with the Two-Ten two-door sedan but featured a quilted all-vinyl interior. Still, 115,584 buyers put down the $1835 Chevy asked for it.

THE NEW NOMAD—Long, low and very different—the car that stole the show at auto shows everywhere—the Nomad is the newest achievement of Chevrolet Station Wagon styling.

Stylish Wagons by Chevrolet!

More and more people are joining the Station-Wagon set—and no wonder, with this spanking quintet of Motoramic Chevrolet wagons to choose from! Beautifully styled inside and out and with space to spare . . . from the luxurious Nomad to the rugged Handy-man, an entirely new concept of stylish low-priced Station Wagons. And every one's as practical as you expect a station wagon to be. See them soon at your Chevrolet dealer's. . . . Chevrolet Division of General Motors, Detroit 2, Mich.

THE "TWO-TEN" HANDYMAN—At work or at play, this 2-door Station Wagon is a pleasure to look at—a joy to drive. Front-seat backs swing way up for easy access to rear seat and cargo area. Interiors—even roof linings—are of colorful, tough and easily washable vinyl.

THE BEL AIR BEAUVILLE—The rakish dash of the Bel Air sport series combines with utility in this sleek 4-door model. Only Chevrolet in the low-price field gives you Sweep-Sight vision, fore and aft—shoulder-to-shoulder windshields and curved rear quarter windows.

THE "TWO-TEN" TOWNSMAN—Rugged and handsome in every detail—because Chevrolet gives you something no other low-priced car can . . . Body by Fisher. Extra tough under the hood, too: your choice of two new "Blue-Flame" 6's or the surging new "Turbo-Fire V8."

THE "ONE-FIFTY" HANDYMAN—Like all Chevrolet Station Wagons, this 2-door boasts more load length than ever —fully ten extra inches, for both rear seat back and cushion fold into the floor. Glide-Ride front suspension and outrigger rear springs give new driving ease.

Stealing the thunder from the high-priced cars!

1955
Bel Air Nomad

Even the utilitarian station wagon couldn't escape the attention of Chevrolet stylists in the 1950s. They borrowed a roof design from a 1954 Motorama show car, opened up the rear wheel wells, striped the tailgate in chrome, and created the Nomad. Though a part of the top-rank Bel Air series, the Nomad featured its own side trim and waffle-pattern upholstery. The two-door configuration sacrificed some convenience, the raked tailgate was prone to leaks, and the Nomad cost $309 more than a four-door Bel Air wagon, so it's little wonder that just 8386 were made. But they are among the most cherished of the more than 1.7 million '55s Chevy made, a total that kept the marque at number 1 in a year of record-setting sales for the U.S. auto industry.

The new Bel Air Sport Sedan (one of two new 4-door hardtops) shown on the Pikes Peak road where Chevrolet broke the record.

Nothing without wings climbs like a '56 Chevrolet !

Aim this new Chevrolet up a steep grade—and you'll see why it's the Pikes Peak record breaker.

Ever level off a mountain with your foot? Just point this new '56 Chevy uphill and ease down on the gas.

In the merest fraction of a second you sense that big bore V8 lengthening out its stride. And up you go with a silken rush of power that makes a mountain seem as flat as a roadmap!

For nothing without wings climbs like a '56 Chevrolet! This is the car, you know, that broke the Pikes Peak record. The car that proved its fired-up performance, cat-sure cornering ability and nailed-down stability on the rugged, twisting Pikes Peak road. And *all* these qualities mean more driving safety and pleasure for you.

THE HOT ONE'S EVEN HOTTER

You'll see that when you *drive* the new Chevrolet. You've 19 frisky new models to choose from, with new higher horsepower—ranging up to a top of 205!

Borrow the key to one at your Chevrolet dealer's. . . . Chevrolet Division of General Motors, Detroit 2, Michigan.

CHEVROLET

Highway-test it— it's a beautiful thing to handle!

1956
Bel Air

Having called its '55 car "The Hot One," Chevrolet posited that the 1956 version was "even hotter." That seemed obvious on paper—the optional four-barrel V8 was rated at 205 hp, and 225 hp was available with twin carbs. (Even the base 6 was beefed up.) For proof, there was this: On September 9, 1955, Zora Arkus-Duntov, Chevy's resident hot-shoe engineer, ran a preproduction '56 up Pikes Peak to an American stock sedan record for the 12.5-mile sprint. Beneath the body extensions and tape stripes designed to foil sneak peeks at the new car during Duntov's run was a Bel Air hardtop sedan. This new body type blended four-door convenience with hardtop style for $2344 as a Bel Air (opposite) or $2117 in Two-Ten trim. About two-thirds of the '56s sold were Bel Airs.

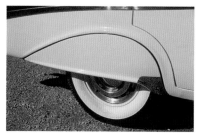

CHEVROLET UNLEASHES THE NEW CORVETTE

Get set for the new Corvette. Get set for a new sight in sports car style and silhouette. Get set for a new sound, a new sensation, a new spirit-lifting surge of the Corvette's dynamic new 225-hp V8 engine. Get set, too, for new Corvette convenience—with new roll-up windows, a custom choice of standard power-operated fabric top or optional convertible hardtop, Powerglide or Synchro-Mesh transmission, and beautiful new colors and interiors. There's more—a new competition racing steering wheel, side-by-side bucket seats, and instrumentation as complete as a light plane's. But excitement is as excitement does. And you'll never know that till you drive it! . . . Chevrolet Division of General Motors, Detroit 2, Mich.

CORVETTE

by Chevrolet

1956
Corvette

Chevrolet's sporty two-seater became an honest-to-goodness sports car in 1956. It was now solely V8 powered, with 210 hp to start or the 225-hp dual-four-barrel version on tap at extra cost. A three-speed floor-shift gearbox—a mid-'55 alternative to the Powerglide automatic found in all early 'Vettes—was now standard. The 225-hp/three-speed combination could launch the slickly restyled car to 60 mph in 7.5 seconds. Roll-up windows and an optional lift-off hardtop improved comfort. What the Corvette wasn't—yet—was a bona fide sales success. Orders for the $3149 car came to just 3467, far better than the 700 made the year before, but well below expectations. Patience on the part of Chevrolet management would prove to be a virtue, though.

SWEET, SMOOTH AND SASSY—the beautiful Bel Air Sport Coupe. You can see and feel the solid quality of its Body by Fisher.

filled with grace and great new things

It looks agile, graceful and easy to handle — and it more than lives up to its looks! Chevy offers fuel injection and America's first and only triple-turbine transmission.

You expect something pretty special in the way of driving pleasure the very first time you take charge of a new Chevrolet. Those clean, graceful contours hold a promise of quicksilver responsiveness. And there's something about the low, action-poised profile that tells you Chevy's a honey to handle.

It doesn't take long to find out that this car lives up to all its "advance notice"—and

then some! Horsepower ranging up to 245* translates your toe-touch into cream-smooth motion. You find that turning a corner is almost as easy as making a wish. And you see how Chevrolet's solid sureness of control makes for safer, happier driving on city streets, superhighways and everything in between.

If you drive a new Chevrolet with Turbo-glide (an extra-cost option), you'll discover triple-turbine takeoff and a new flowing kind of going.

Stop by your Chevrolet dealer's and sample *all* these great new things! . . . Chevrolet Division of General Motors, Detroit 2, Mich.

*270-h.p. high-performance engine also available at extra cost. Ram Jet fuel injection engines with up to 283 h.p. in Corvette and passenger car models.

1957
Bel Air

In its day, the 1957 Chevrolet had to settle for second place in the sales race behind Ford. Since then, though, it has become a clear number 1 among car buffs. The one everybody wants is a Bel Air. In its last go-round on the 1955 body shells, the Bel Air came in seven body styles, including the final two-door Nomad. All '57 Chevys featured a freshened face with more deeply hooded headlights and twin windsplits on the hood. Rear quarter panels ended in pointed finlike extensions. Bel Airs were set apart from lesser models by an anodized filler for the side trim, rocker-panel brightwork, gold-toned front-fender hashmarks, and more-colorful interiors. There was excitement under the hood, too: a small-block V8 enlarged to 283 cid was available for every 1957 Chevy.

TOWARD AN AMERICAN CLASSIC . . . THE 1957 CORVETTE WITH FUEL INJECTION! It is with considerable pride that Chevrolet invites you to examine an engineering advance of great significance, available on the 1957 Corvette. It is fuel injection, and in the Corvette V8 it permits a level of efficiency hitherto unrealized in any American production car: *one horsepower for every cubic inch of displacement . . . 283 h.p.!* In addition, there is unprecedented responsiveness, even during warm-up; virtually instantaneous acceleration and significant gains in overall gas economy.

This is another major step in the creation of a proud new kind of car for America: a *genuine* sports car, as certified by its record in competition. But a *unique* sports car in its combination of moderate price, luxurious equipment and low-cost maintenance with fiery performance, polo-pony responsiveness and granite stability on curves.

It is our intention to make of the Corvette a classic car, one of those rare and happy milestones in the history of automotive design. We take pleasure in inviting you to drive the 1957 version—and see just how close we have come to the target. . . . *Chevrolet Division of General Motors, Detroit 2, Michigan.*

CORVETTE
by Chevrolet

SPECIFICATIONS: 283-cubic-inch V8 engine with single four-barrel carburetor, 220 h.p. (four other engines* range to 283 h.p. with fuel injection). Close-ratio three-speed manual transmission standard, with special Powerglide automatic drive* available on all but maximum-performance engines. Choice of removable hard top or power-operated fabric top, Power-Lift windows.* Instruments include 6000 r.p.m. tachometer, oil pressure gauge and ammeter. *Optional at extra cost.

1957
Corvette

Though its 1956 restyling had made the Corvette an undeniably attractive sports car, the real beauty of the follow-up '57 model truly was more than skin deep. All 'Vettes had the new 283-cid engine under their front-hinged hoods, and a few of them came with fuel injection. Carbureted Corvette engines made 220, 245, and 270 hp, the last two with twin four-barrels. Rochester Products' "Ramjet" mechanical fuel injection boosted output to 250 hp with hydraulic lifters or 283—one horsepower per cubic inch—with mechanical lifters. (The "fuelie" engines were also offered in Chevy family cars.) As if that wasn't enough of a good thing, a four-speed manual transmission became optional in May. A four-speed/283-hp Corvette could go from 0 to 60 mph in six seconds or less.

YOU'LL GET A REAL CHARGE *out of the way this* **'58 CHEVROLET** *responds to your touch, the slightest hint of command. Here's vigorous new V8 performance that's enough to perk up anybody's pride. Here's quick, eager-to-please handling that lets you know you're the boss, right from the start!*

That's a wonderful feeling, you know. But it doesn't happen by chance; it's a careful blend of qualities that demands real engineering talent.

Very few cars in any price range even come close to Chevy's precise, clean ease of handling, the beautifully balanced way it clings to any road, the crisp accuracy of its steering, the supple sure-footedness of its Full Coil suspension.

There's never been another list of tremendous advances like the '58

Chevrolet's Level Air 100 percent air springs*, its low-slung X-built frame, its unprecedented Turbo-Thrust V8 engines*, its totally new bodies. But the biggest advance in the new Chevrolet is the whole new feeling of ease and competence and security. You won't know how significant *that* is till you try it—and that's something you ought to do this week! . . . *Chevrolet Division of General Motors, Detroit 2, Michigan.*   *Optional at extra cost.*

1958
Bel Air Impala

When medium-priced cars enjoyed a boost in popularity in the mid '50s, executives for the low-priced makes decided to emulate them. In Chevrolet's case, it took until 1958 to come out with cars that were bigger, heavier, cushier, and more powerful. Wheelbase stretched out to 117.5 inches on an all-new X-frame chassis that adopted rear coil springs—or the option of four-wheel air suspension. The 6-cylinder and 283-cid V8 engine lineup was augmented by a new 348-cube V8 with combustion chambers in the block. It made 250 to 315 hp depending on the setup. "Sculpturamic" styling featured quad headlights, "jet-intake" parking lights, and canted rear fenders. The Bel Air added a flashy subseries, a hardtop coupe and convertible with a name destined for greatness: Impala.

Brand new...and bred for action!

This is a very special car for special people with very particular requirements. We'll grant you it is as sleekly handsome a machine as ever whispered down a boulevard, with an individual flair that is shared by no other. And we'll also concede that its road manners are impeccable, that it moves with a glove-leather suppleness that is obedience personified. But the real difference between the 1958 Corvette and any other American car is this: It is an authentic sports car. Under that wind-sculptured shape is a superb

corvette for '58

CORVETTE
by Chevrolet

sports car chassis with almost incredible road-holding and balance; under that low-raked hood is a sports car V8 with almost incredible urge and capacity. You think "incredible" is too strong a word?...Try it and see!...*Chevrolet Division of General Motors, Detroit 2, Michigan.*

1958
Corvette

The 1958 Corvette might have had an aluminum body and unitized construction. It might have been a finned coupe inspired by the Oldsmobile Golden Rocket Motorama show car. Instead, it remained a fiberglass-body-on-frame convertible that evolved from the 1956–57 design. Though wheelbase stayed at 102 inches long, overall length and width increased. So did weight, which bothered sports car purists. Neither were they enthralled with all of the styling updates, which included quad headlights, outboard grille "nostrils," faux hood louvers, and twin chrome strips on the decklid. (The louvers and deck trim would be dropped for '59.) To the good was a redesigned instrument panel. Engine choices stood pat, but the base mill was up to 230 hp, and the top fuelie now made 290.

The Bel Air 4-Door Sedan with a roomier Body by Fisher.

NOTHING'S NEW
LIKE CHEVY'S NEW!

Impala Sport Coupe—new down to its tougher Tyrex cord tires.

From the winging shape of its saucy rear deck to the simple elegance of its grille, this car shows you it's new in a decidedly different way. You get more of what you want—more spacious interiors, vast new areas of visibility, a longer lasting finish and all the solid virtues of economy and practicality you've come to expect in a Chevy.

One look at this '59 Chevrolet tells you here's a car with a whole new slant on driving. You see the transformation in its low-set headlights, the overhead curve of its windshield, the sheen of its longer lasting Magic-Mirror acrylic finish.

But to discover all that's fresh and fine you must relax in Chevy's wider seats, feel the loungelike comfort of its new interior, experience the hushed tranquillity of its ride.

You'll also find bigger brakes, a new 6 that gets up to 10 percent more miles a gallon and vim-packed V8's.

Your Chevrolet dealer's waiting now to show you the car that's shaped to the new American taste. . . . Chevrolet Division of General Motors, Detroit 2, Michigan.

*What America wants,
America gets in a Chevy!*

1959
Bel Air

Chevrolet's push for longer, lower, and wider cars continued in '59 under dramatic new sheetmetal. With wheelbase stretched again to 119 inches, Chevys were now an even 210 inches bumper-to-bumper and 2.2 inches wider at 79.9. Styling featured high-riding gullwing fins over "cat's-eye" taillights, headlights set at grille height, and airy rooflines with more glass. Though the 6 was detuned for added economy, horsepower ratings for the 348 V8 were up to 335 hp. A four-speed stickshift was newly available, but fuel injection and air suspension put in their final appearances as family car options. The Impala expanded to full-series status, so the Bel Air became the midlevel line. It was offered in three body styles including a four-door sedan (opposite) with a starting price of $2440.

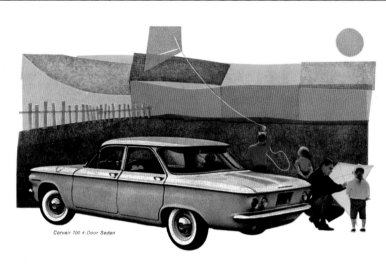

Corvair 700 4-Door Sedan

Light-handed, light-footed, light-hearted!

Even though a Corvair's main virtues are economy and efficiency, we're willing to wager the thing which sends you away singing from your first drive is the way it *handles*. Only rear-engine design gives you steering that is so light and responsive, traction that is so solid and reassuring, braking so beautifully balanced front and rear. This is a light-hearted car, because it does everything so crisply and so easily; light-footed because there's *independent* suspension at all four wheels; light-handed because the steering doesn't have to cope with the weight of a front engine. But try it yourself—and find a completely new dimension in driving!

A magician on mileage. *Your gas dollars will now go farther . . . because the Corvair delivers miles and miles and miles per gallon.*

Engine's in the rear...*where it belongs in a compact car . . . to give you nimbler handling, greater traction, better 4-wheel braking.*

Unipack power team. *Wraps engine, transmission and drive gears into one compact package . . . takes less room, leaves you more.*

Independent suspension at all 4 wheels. *Coil springs at each and every wheel take bumps with independent knee-action for a ride that rivals the costliest cars.*

Fold-down rear seat. *Now every Corvair converts into a station wagon with 17.6 cu. ft. of extra storage space behind front seat.*

Choice of automatic or manual transmission. *You can have Powerglide* or a smooth-shifting Synchro-Mesh standard transmission.*

*Optional at extra cost

Four models. *Practical four-door or sleek new two-door in standard or de luxe versions.*

Trunk's up front. *Plenty of luggage space under the hood, where it's convenient to get to.*

All at a practical kind of price. *Check your dealer on the short, sweet details....Chevrolet Division of General Motors, Detroit 2, Michigan.*

the happiest driving compact car ★

corvair
by Chevrolet

Corvair 700 5-Passenger Club Coupe

1960
Corvair

When the post-World War II trickle of economical imported small cars into the USA became a steady stream by the mid '50s, domestic automakers committed themselves to creating compacts of their own. General Motors' first such car was the 1960 Chevrolet Corvair. Division General Manager Edward Cole wanted to take on the leading import—Volkswagen—so he backed a design with an air-cooled "boxer" engine in the rear, VW's signature feature. The Corvair's aluminum-block 6 displaced 140 cubic inches and made 80 hp. Independent swing axles supported the rear. The 108-inch-wheelbase unit-body Corvair made its debut as a four-door sedan in two trim levels. Coupes in 500- and 700-series (opposite) trim arrived in January and a Monza with a bucket-seat interior in May.

1960
Nomad

Two things grew together in postwar "baby-boom" America: the size of families and the demand for station wagons. For 1960, Chevrolet offered shoppers a thorough wagon lineup. Chevy wagons provided up to 92 cubic feet of cargo space. Though a separate series, they shadowed the passenger cars' exterior and interior trim, starting with the Biscayne-like Brookwood two- and four-door models. The six-passenger Parkwood and nine-seat Kingswood, both four-doors, matched the Bel Air. At the top of the pack sat the four-door, six-place Nomad with Impala-grade gear. It sold for $2889 with a 6 or $2996 with the base 283-cid V8. Though still finny, styling was toned down from the year before. Taillights reverted to round lenses as seen in 1958. Side trim adopted jet motifs.

1961
Impala

Chevrolet stylists bade goodbye to fins on the totally restyled '61 bodies that were shorter and narrower than before. Meanwhile, division engineers spurred on the accelerating horsepower race with a new high-performance V8. The crisply creased styling looked particularly good on the five Impala models. (A two-door sedan was added for this year only.) Better yet for the leadfoot set, they could all be ordered with a new Super Sport option that included suspension and brake upgrades, narrow-band whitewall tires, and SS identification. Super Sports came only with 348 V8s of 305, 340, and 350 hp, or a new 409-cid engine that made 360 hp. All but the 305-hp mill required a four-speed transmission. With a 4.56:1 axle, a 409 could run the quarter-mile in just over 14 seconds.

LUXURIOUS LIVELINESS AT A LOW, LOW PRICE

1962
Chevy II

Despite the daring unconventionality of the Corvair (or perhaps *because* of it), Chevrolet leaders quickly realized it wouldn't be as popular as the rival Ford Falcon. The answer, they thought, was a more-mainstream small car. Just 18 months after the start of design work, the Chevy II came out as a 1962 model. The 110-inch-wheelbase cars featured unitized body construction with "Mono-Plate" single-leaf springs in back. A 153-cid 4—Chevy's first since 1928—and a 194-cid 6 were underhood. Styling borrowed a few hints from the big cars. The 100 and 300 series offered only sedans and station wagons, while the exclusively 6-cylinder Nova 400 series added a sporty hardtop and convertible. Model-year orders totaled 326,607—less than Falcon but more than Corvair.

NON-MECHANICAL MEN

ARISE!

There's a cult of sports-car-type people who spread the myth that one needs vast knowledge of things mechanical to own a sports car. Be not deceived! This may be true of some machines, but not the Corvette. Any Corvette, however equipped, will give unruffled, unfussy driving pleasure while outperforming cars that cost three times as much and require the full-time attention of a bilingual mechanic. No, friends, if you yearn to spend long hours lying on cold cement, covered with grease, shop elsewhere. Corvettes are for driving; fill them with gas and people and point them down the road. That's the way to enjoy this automobile! Of course, if you simply must do something, we don't mind if you wash it yourself. (Radio, as shown, optional at extra cost.) . . . Chevrolet Division of General Motors, Detroit 2, Mich.

CORVETTE BY CHEVROLET

1962
Corvette

Anyone who liked the 1958 Corvette should have loved the '62. They shared basic styling, a wraparound windshield, centered gauges, and a solid rear axle. To this the latter model offered an upsized small-block V8 bored and stroked to 327 cid and offered in four horsepower ratings from 250 to 360, the latter with optional fuel injection. The 1962 'Vette continued the "ducktail" rear styling and round taillights first seen in 1961, but did away with the side-cove two-toning option. A heater became standard equipment. Though the Corvette's base price inched past $4000 for the first time, production came to 14,531 for the model year, a new high for the fiberglass flier. It was a rousing send-off for the first generation of Chevy's sports car; waiting in the wings was a sensational new version.

1962
Impala

In its few short years on the market, the Impala, Chevrolet's plushest and most stylish family car, had become the industry's biggest sales force. In '62, when the division claimed 30 percent of the market, production of its full-sized cars alone came to more than 1.4 million. Of that number, 52 percent were Impalas. In terms of appearance, front and rear edges were more squared off than in '61 and the signature six tail-lights sat in an aluminum-covered cove. Hard-top coupes got a roof that looked like a raised convertible top. Inside was a new two-spoke steering wheel. Bucket seats and a console were offered for Super Sports. With small-block 327 V8s added to the lineup, the 348s were cut. The 409 now made 380 hp with a single four-barrel caburetor or 409 hp with dual carbs.

ONLY A MAN WITH A HEART OF STONE COULD WITHSTAND TEMPTATION LIKE THIS. You can wear a blindfold, have your wife tie you to the old family sedan, lock up the checkbook, anything of the kind; but Mister, if you ever hankered to buy a sports car, you're about to become the owner of a new Corvette Sting Ray. Sensible talk about the family budget, the good years left in your present car, any kind of rational thought, forget it! Here's why: The new Corvette Sting Ray, available in sport coupe or traditional convertible model, takes all the excellent characteristics of earlier Corvettes and multiplies them by two. The previous Corvette was the world's most exciting sports car for the last five years, and this new one shows every indication of keeping the title for the *next* five. It has fully independent rear suspension, bigger self-adjusting brakes, retractable headlights, a V8 engine that's prettier than most girls, and new extra-cost options like a four-speed all-synchro transmission, knock-off aluminum wheels, monstrous finned aluminum brake drums with metallic linings, and Fuel Injection for 360 horsepower. Combine all this with a seating position and a seat-of-the-pants driving sensation like nothing you ever felt, and you've got a car that absolutely will not be denied. And if you're interested enough to have read all this, you might as well stop by the bank on your way to the Chevrolet dealer's. It's fate, man. . . . Chevrolet Division of General Motors, Detroit 2, Mich.

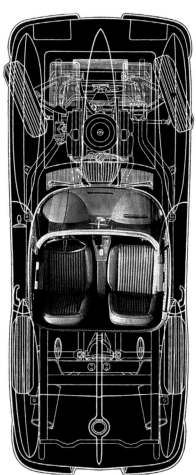

New CORVETTE Sting Ray by Chevrolet

1963
Corvette Sting Ray

To say the 1963 Corvette was an all-new car barely scratches the surface. It featured completely different styling, an independent rear suspension, the addition of a coupe body, and it even picked up a new name. The styling is considered a highlight of Bill Mitchell's 1958–77 tenure as GM design chief. Hidden headlights went on to be a Corvette "must" for decades, and the coupe's split rear window—a '63-only touch—became iconic. Corvette Chief Engineer Zora Arkus-Duntov picked out a new ladder frame, a wheelbase pared to 98 inches, and a frame-mounted differential from which extended axle halfshafts connected by U-joints. Weight was cut and balance was improved. The buying public approved. Production came to 10,594 coupes and 10,919 convertibles.

'63 Chevrolet Impala Convertible—Smoothest way to top off a tour of San Francisco

Most comfortable thing since grandmother's lap

Driving ease and creature comfort are the top considerations for most new car buyers. They have a lot of places to travel to, and they want to get there with maximum comfort and minimum effort. That's what you get with any Jet-smooth 1963 Chevrolet, be it a Biscayne, Bel Air, or an Impala like the one in the picture. Chevrolet's Jet-smooth ride whisks you away from home for a weekend, or delivers you briskly to the market in regal splendor never before offered by a car in this class. A look at the *outside* of that crisp, gleaming Body by Fisher assures you of unending comfort and quiet. A turn of the key and a touch of the throttle prove it.

This new Chevrolet is the doggonedest collection of automotive virtues ever assembled under one nameplate. For example, the air-washed flush-and-dry rocker panels, the marvelous system that takes rain water and air from the cowl to rinse away corrosion-causing elements. The Delcotron generator, working quietly and without fuss, to help keep a more-than-ample supply of electrical current on hand and extend the life of your battery. We could go on like this until tomorrow, but really, very little of it will mean much to you, until you drive one. It's a remarkable car, even for Chevrolet Division of General Motors, Detroit 2, Mich.

The make more people depend on

1963
Impala

Impala's winning formula was refined for '63, beginning with touched-up styling on the 1961 body shells. Key points included a grille inspired by the '61 Cadillac, front window posts straightened at their bases, a pronounced low-body crease capped by a paint-filled trim spear, and a slightly modified four-door hardtop roof. Base engines were a new-design 6—a 230-cid unit of 140 hp—and a 195-hp 283 V8. Options included a pair of 327s and a trio of 409s. A 340-hp hydraulic-lifter 409 joined the stouter mechanical-lifter jobs, which now made 400 and 425 hp. Alternators replaced generators. Impala starting prices ran from $2661 to $3170. A total of 153,271 customers spent an additional $161.40 to add Super Sport gear to their Impala two-door hardtop or convertible (opposite).

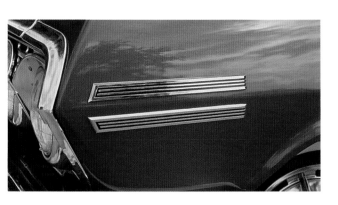

Chevelle Malibu Super Sport Coupe (all this and bucket seats, too !)

WE DIDN'T JUST MAKE CHEVELLE BEAUTIFUL AND HOPE FOR THE BEST

You might want Chevelle just because you like its looks. But if you think all we had in mind was a good-looking car smaller than Chevrolet and bigger than Chevy II, read on.

One of the most beautiful things about Chevelle is the way it fits between parking meters (with five feet left over), yet still has a Fisher Body-ful of room inside.

Think those curved side windows are only for looks? They slant in for easy entry, and don't need bulky space-wasting doors to roll down into.

Chevelle's long wide hood looks nice, too. But it's that way because of what goes under it—things like a wide choice of Six and V8 engines, not to mention extra-cost air conditioning and anything else you'd like us to put there.

Chevelle's rear deck is just a smart cover-up for a 27.3-cu.-ft. trunk. (In case you haven't cubed a foot lately, it can hold 4 overnight bags, 2 two-suiters, 2 pullmans, 1 wardrobe and 1 train case, with a set of golf clubs thrown in for good measure.)

We've been very practical about the whole thing. If you think like we do, you're practically driving one already.... Chevrolet Division of General Motors, Detroit, Michigan.

Chevrolet • Chevelle • Chevy II • Corvair • Corvette

THE GREAT HIGHWAY PERFORMERS

CHEVELLE! BY CHEVROLET

1964
Chevelle

Between the so-called standards and the compacts there was room for another class of car: the intermediate. General Motors plunged into this fairly new market in a big way in 1964, pumping up the existing compacts from Pontiac, Oldsmobile, and Buick and introducing the Chevrolet Chevelle. The new midsize Chevys were up to 16 inches shorter than their full-sized companions and 3.5 inches narrower. Chevelle's 115-inch wheelbase matched that of the fondly recalled "shoebox" Chevys of the '50s. The chassis featured all-coil suspension. Engine choices comprised two 6s, two 283 V8s, and—late—a pair of 327s. Series were the base 300, nicer Malibu, and sporty Malibu SS (opposite). With the Chevelle-based El Camino pickup, seven body styles were offered.

1964
Biscayne

The highly popular Impala met many buyers' needs for room and creature comforts at an affordable price. Some customers, though, wanted the Impala's space and power at a greater savings. The Biscayne was made for them. The name first appeared on a Motorama car in 1955 before replacing Two-Ten as the midlevel nameplate in '58. The following year, it was pushed down to entry-level status, where it stayed through 1972. Available '64 body types were two- and four-door sedans and a station wagon. Simply trimmed sedan interiors featured cloth-and-vinyl upholstery. Prices averaged $230 less than comparable Impala models. Any engine and transmission found in Impalas could be ordered for Biscaynes, including the 425-hp 409 V8 and manual four-speed.

'65 Chevrolet Impala Sport Coupe—pamperer

Some cars pamper passengers.
Some cars pamper drivers.
Chevrolet pampers both.

**Foam-cushioned seats and deep-twist carpeting underfoot—you passengers have it made.
So do you drivers with new engines, transmissions and Wide-Stance handling.
Now everybody's happy—have a great trip!**

List the things your next-car should have. Then watch this Impala tick them off.

Comfort and luxury? The Chevrolet Impala starts out lavish and goes from there. Carpeting that runs all over the place. Vinyl upholstery surrounded by tufted pattern cloth. An electric clock with a sweep-second hand. An instrument panel with the look of hand-rubbed walnut. Armrests. Personal touches you can order, like air conditioning, tinted glass, AM/FM Stereo radio and a Comfortilt steering wheel.

Ride and handling? You came to the right place. Chevrolet's improved Full Coil suspension and new Wide-Stance tread design make use of every engineering advance available. That Jet-smooth ride is better than ever! And one long stretch of road is all that is needed to have you discover the difference.

Performance? You can order a wide choice of power, beginning with the 140-hp Six and ranging up to Chevrolet's new 396-cubic-inch Turbo-Jet V8.

Two new transmissions available, too: the Turbo-Hydra-Matic, a liquid-smooth new automatic transmission for quicker highway passing and quieter cruising; and a new *fully synchronized* 3-Speed.

Price? Nice. It's an old Chevrolet custom. . . . Chevrolet Division of General Motors, Detroit, Michigan.

1965
Impala

Chevy's full-sized cars were completely new for 1965, starting with a perimeter frame with wider front and rear tracks, and topped by sleek new styling. There were new power team choices and a luxury interior and trim option that turned an Impala four-door hardtop into a Caprice. Styling featured a kick-up feature atop the rear quarters and curved side-window glass. Impala and Impala SS (a stand-alone series since '64) hardtops cleanly broke with the recent past via a sloping semifastback roof. The '65s were available in 15 colors, the most distinctive being a light-violet metallic called Evening Orchid. A 250-cid 6 and a 396-cid V8 arrived during the model year, replacing the 230- and 409-cube engines. A fully synchronized three-speed and Turbo Hydra-Matic transmissions were new.

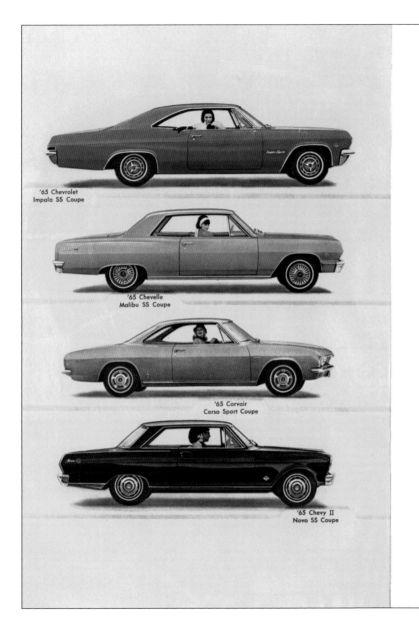

'65 Chevrolet
Impala SS Coupe

'65 Chevelle
Malibu SS Coupe

'65 Corvair
Corsa Sport Coupe

'65 Chevy II
Nova SS Coupe

Let Chevrolet put you
in beautiful shape for '65

Now, a Chevrolet that makes everything over, under and around you beautifully different. A completely new Corvair with its first big change in five years. A Chevelle that doesn't hold back on anything but cost. And a Chevy II that's turned into the most powerful tightwad in town!

For 1965, the big luxurious Chevrolet could almost get by on looks alone. But that's far from all that's new.

It's longer, lower, roomier, heavier, more luxurious than any Chevrolet before. Completely new from the sleek Impala Super Sport Coupe roof line all the way down to the Jet-smooth suspension.

More expensive looking outside, richer looking inside, more shoulder room, more leg room up front — all in all, we think it's the *best* Chevrolet we've ever built.

'65 Corvair

Corvair's rear engine has never had so much excitement to look forward to. Inside, there's more shoulder room. More comfort. The effortless handling only a

rear engine and new independent suspension can give.

All wrapped up in seven models, including the brand-new top-of-the-line Corsa.

New performance, too—up to 180 hp that you can order in the Corsa Series.

Wait till the ones who always wait till next year see this!

'65 Chevelle

There are enough changes in Chevelle to make it, too, feel like another whole new car from Chevrolet.

New ride, new style, and an engine that will make *you* feel young again — a 300-hp V8 that you can order in all twelve Chevelles.

And its smoother ride and extra body insulation make things as quiet as the day the kids went back to school.

And if that's too quiet, order an AM-FM Stereo radio.

'65 Chevy II

Our economy is on the upswing!

For '65, Chevy II has a dressed-up front, back, interior and a smart new roof on sedans. Plus two new V8's available: a 250-hp and a 300-hp.

Underlying it, though, are those things that have made Chevy II such a tightwad these past years.

And as your Chevrolet dealer will show you, Chevy II's now the most *exciting* tightwad in town. . . . Chevrolet Division of General Motors, Detroit, Michigan.

1965
Corvair

After five seasons in its original body configuration, the rear-engine Corvair was ready for a restyling. The new look, attributed to designer Ron Hill, featured seductive Italianate lines. All closed cars were now pillarless hardtops. The new theme would see the Corvair through the end of its life in 1969. The number of series was reduced for '65. A 500, Monza, and Corsa were offered at prices that ran from $2066 for the 500 two-door hardtop to $2665 for the Corsa convertible. A true independent rear suspension fully tamed past handling woes. Flat 6s of 95 and 110 hp were carried over from 1964. The Corsa (right) came with a standard 140-hp normally aspirated engine or a turbocharged 180-hp optional job that could launch the car to 60 mph in 9.5 seconds.

Chevy II Nova Super Sport Coupe

Chevy II Super Sport by Chevrolet
The car that makes economy exciting!

A bright red all-vinyl interior. Bucket seats. A sporty instrument panel.
You'll never know how economical it is until you own one.

Deep down this Chevy II Super Sport may be one of the big-time savers, but you'd never know it by the way it looks and acts.

For behind every battery-saving Delcotron generator, there's foam-cushioned bucket-seated luxury.

Above every aluminized exhaust system, there's a network of thick deep-twist carpeting.

For every set of self-adjusting brakes with bonded linings, there's an electric clock with a sweep second hand.

For every flush-and-dry rocker panel system, there's a sporty, easy-to-read instrument panel with a sunshine-bright trim.

For every nine-step acrylic lacquer finish and rugged Body by Fisher, there are things like color-keyed seat belts and all-vinyl trim.

For every squeak-proof single-leaf rear spring, there are exciting accessories to order like an AM-FM *Stereo* radio.

For every set of protective steel inner fenders, there's a wide choice of engines and four different transmissions you may order.

But why don't you see for yourself just how exciting economy can get. Test-drive a Chevy II Super Sport today.

Be a real sport and a real tightwad all at the same time. . . . Chevrolet Division of General Motors, Detroit, Michigan.

1965
Chevy II Nova SS

The successful Super Sport concept pioneered by the Impala was extended to the Chevy II Nova in 1963. The loss of a Nova convertible in '64 was offset by the first-time availability of V8 power and the remaining SS hardtop's ascension to series status. That set the stage for the 1965 model—the last to appear with the original Chevy II body—9100 of which were built. Though a 6 was still standard for the Nova SS in '65, a whole slew of V8s was available. A 195-hp 283 started things off, but a new 220-hp version with a four-barrel carburetor and dual exhausts turned up the heat. Then, later in the year, 250- and 300-hp 327s were added. New grille and taillight designs updated the '65s. The $2433 base price bought special trim and wheel covers, plus bucket seats and a console.

Caprice Custom Coupe with Strato-bucket seats and center console you can order

'66 CAPRICE BY CHEVROLET

More than an elegant new car,

it's a luxurious new series:

four models in all. The Caprice Customs,

made by Chevrolet.

Coupe, Sedan and Wagons now. And elegance is everywhere you turn. Rich fabrics. Supple vinyls. Deep-twist carpeting underfoot. The look of hand-rubbed walnut.

For the Coupe, there's a rakish new roof line you won't see on any other Chevrolet. Slender new Strato-bucket seats and center console, on order. Wagons—two-seat and three—have the look of wood along each side and in back.

Caprice rides so hushed and steady, you'll think you're gliding *above* the road instead of on it. As for performance, we offer all you'd ask: Turbo-Jet 427, for one, a 390-hp V8 that's smooth and quiet. Caprice: not the car for everyone, but maybe the car for *you*. See, at your Chevrolet dealer's.

Chevrolet Division of General Motors, Detroit, Michigan

80

1966
Caprice

Chevy's efforts to make its cars more upscale took another step with the Caprice. From a $200 option package in 1965, it expanded into a stand-alone three-car series for '66. The previously available four-door hardtop was now joined by a two-door hardtop and a station wagon with a choice of two- or three-row seating. Situated atop the family car price structure, the tab started at $3000 for the hardtop coupe, with its distinctive Cadillac-inspired roofline, and ran to $3347 for a three-seat wagon with imitation wood on the sides. Extra sound insulation, plusher foam-cushioned seats, and woodgrain interior detailing were included. The 195-hp 283 V8 was standard in Caprices. The new top engine choice was a 427-cid V8 (a bored-out version of the 396) in 390- and 425-hp ratings.

'66 CHEVELLE

It's different inside and out, as you can see.
And this Chevelle's the newest of all: Super Sport 396!

Now for 1966, Chevelle Super Sport is all this: new 325-hp Turbo-Jet V8, special suspension, fully synchronized 3-speed with floor-mounted shifter, special hood and emblems, red stripe tires—packaged as sport coupe or convertible. Or you can order 360 hp in an SS 396.

Of course, there's still a Turbo-Fire V8 or a thrifty Six for anyone who mostly likes the look and luxury and comfort Chevelle ladles out in

10 other models. New styling, headlights to taillamps. All-new interiors. A jaunty new roof line for the coupes. A handsome new 4-door hardtop: the Malibu Sport Sedan.

What we haven't changed is Chevelle's Full Coil-springed ride. Its stretchout roominess. Its middle-sized handling ease. You'll see, Chevelle for 1966 goes more beautifully than ever between Chevrolet and Chevy II.

CHEVROLET

Chevelle Super Sport 396 Coupe with Strato-bucket seats and console you can order—See lots more. Turn the page . . .

1966
Chevelle SS 396

The 1960s muscle car boom that began with the Impala SS and others of that ilk reached full strength when it spread to the intermediates. The right combination of light bodies and mighty engines made for some of the most remarkable cars of the decade. Chevrolet's entry in this field was the Chevelle SS 396. Though still set on the original Chevelle chassis, the '66 featured sleek new styling with an eager, forward-leaning front profile and a "flying-buttress" two-door-hardtop roof with a recessed rear window. The SS was now packaged exclusively with the big-block 396 V8; 325 hp was standard, but 360 and 375 were available. With the rare 375-hp engine, the SS 396 could turn a 14.40-second quarter-mile. Some 72,300 Chevelle SS 396 hardtops and convertibles were built.

Corvette Sting Ray Coupe with eight safety features now standard, including two-speed electric wipers for better vision in the worst weather.

In Europe Corvette is a high-priced imported sports car.

Ah, the high-priced imported sports car! Mere mention of the phrase conjures visions of the exotic, the forbidden: of wild forays into the night; of secret agents and clandestine gatherings; of howling engines and winding roads. It must indeed rank as one of man's greatest desires, suppressed or otherwise.

Few, however, realize that Corvette is just such an animal. Some Europeans do, and gladly pay upwards of ten thousand dollars for one.

And frankly we don't blame them. These people have a deucedly sharp eye for Grand Touring machines, and they know Corvette compares feature for feature, spec for spec with Europe's finest.

In fact, with four wheel disc brakes, fully independent suspension and up to 425 horsepower available under the bonnet, we think the Corvette would be quite a buy at 10 thousand. At around five thousand, it's a steal. And that, duty-free, is about what it costs over here where it's built, depending on equipment.

Aren't you glad you live near the factory?

GM

'66 CORVETTE BY CHEVROLET

1966
Corvette Sting Ray

The addition of big-block V8s transformed Corvettes in the mid '60s. The release of an optional 396-cube engine partway through the 1965 model year not only rendered the fuelie 327 obsolete, but it made 'Vettes brutally fast. While heavier than a small-block engine, the big mill did bring weight distribution closer to the ideal 50-percent-front/50-percent-rear split. The 396 was replaced for '66 by the new 427-cid engine with 390- and 425-hp ratings—both considered to be on the conservative side. One magazine test of a 427 'Vette posted a 4.8-second 0-60 sprint and a 140-mph top speed. More than 10,000 of the record 27,720 Corvettes made for '66 had the 427. Four-wheel disc brakes were standard (a '65 change). Purposeful side exhausts were a $131.65 option.

Camaro SS : One to go, with everything.

If Camaro SS were a hamburger, it'd come with mustard, catsup, onion, dill pickles, lettuce, tomato, a side of fries and a garnish of parsley.

But Camaro SS is a road machine and this is how it comes. Lean Camaro styling. A 396-cu.-in. V8 you can order with 325 hp, or the 350 with 295 hp. Red-stripe tires on 14″ x 6″ wheels. You sit in a slim Strato-bucket seat, looking out over

the special louver-styled hood that sports bold color striping around the nose. All this is standard on Camaro SS, with background music by dual exhausts. Would you like to order now?

1967
Camaro

Perhaps the most exciting product in Chevrolet showrooms in 1967 was the newest one: the Camaro, GM's answer to the immensely successful Ford Mustang. Like the original "ponycar," Camaro hardtop coupes and convertibles sported long-hood/short-deck styling and offered lots of comfort and convenience options. The 108.1-inch-wheelbase cars used unit bodies with a front stub frame. Engine selections started with a pair of 6s and two 327 V8s. SS models (opposite) came with a big-block 396 or a new 350-cid small-block V8 added later. A Z-28 package with a special 302-cube V8 made the Camaro eligible for the Trans-Am racing series. Production was about half of Mustang output, but the long-running Ford-Chevy rivalry entered an exciting new phase.

SS 427
For the man who'd buy a sports car if it had this much room

For one thing, you want a sporting kind of engine. In this case, it's a 385-horsepower 427-cubic-inch Turbo-Jet V8, and it's standard SS 427 equipment. Sometimes, when you're not busy, you just like to sit and listen to it idle.

You like a hood that bulges. After all, you've got quite an engine under there, and you don't mind a bit if people know it. In fact, you like things that are distinctive and you know that by its very markings, the SS 427 stands apart from ordinary automobiles.

You want your car to express you just so. And happily, there's a long list of personalized touches you can add to the SS 427 — items like a new 8-track stereo tape system, front disc brakes, 4 speeds forward. Models include a Sport Coupe or Convertible.

You like to unwind. So you really dig the SS 427's stiffer springs, shocks and front stabilizer bar; you know they make for better cornering. The red stripe tires mounted on the extra-wide rims help, too. All of this is standard, of course.

You're a safety-minded individual. You like the idea of the new GM-developed energy-absorbing steering column on Chevrolets. You appreciate the front seat belt retractors and the folding front seat back latches — all standard.

You especially appreciate a dual master cylinder brake system — with a warning light to advise you of a pressure imbalance in either part of the system. You're glad that all other '67 Chevrolets carry the system, too, along with corrosion-resistant brake lines.

Everything new that could happen...*happened* in styling, safety, performance

New Chevrolet SS 427 Sport Coupe (Convertible, too) now performing at your Chevrolet dealer's.

'67 CHEVROLET

1967
Impala SS 427

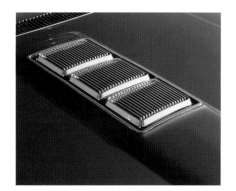

Chevrolet's performance-packaging trend that began with the Chevelle SS 396 came on big in 1967. *Really* big. Impala big. Buyers of Impala Super Sport two-door hardtops and convertibles could get everything from a 155-hp 250-cid 6 to a 325-hp 396 V8. For those who found that still wasn't enough, an outlay of $403.30 would secure a car with SS 427 equipment. As the name suggested, a 427-cid V8 was under the hood. It delivered 385 hp (though a special-order 425-hp job was available, too). Also included were stiffer springs, shock absorbers, and front stabilizer bar; red-stripe tires; and a domed hood with chrome faux intake ports. Front disc brakes were a significant new option. The restyled '67 Impala Super Sport series generated 76,055 orders, 2124 with SS 427 gear.

1967
Chevelle

The Chevelle remained the top-selling mid-size car in America for 1967, but it did so with demand off by 10.6 percent to 369,133. The slip wasn't from lack of effort. The debut of the Camaro in the same dealerships no doubt stole sales from the sportier Chevelle styles. Then, too, the line was getting by on a second-year facelift—albeit an attractive one—in advance of an all-new Chevelle. The grille, reshaped hood, and visibility-enhancing wraparound taillights were highlights of the appearance changes. A premium Concours wagon with woodgrained side trim joined the line. The SS 396 (opposite) suffered some erosion of popularity, losing about 9200 sales for '67. Just a handful of 375-hp cars were built, but front disc brakes were added to the options list.

You can get economy plain or fancy.
So why not fancy?

Nova SS Sport Coupe with a list of safety features longer than the paragraph below.

Why drive something plain as a cast iron skillet? For economy? Ridiculous. Allow us to rattle off some of Chevy II's virtues in this area: A Magic-Mirror acrylic lacquer finish already waxed and polished when you buy it. Rocker panels that clean themselves of rust causers. A long long life battery. A solid solid Body by Fisher. Up to 6,000 miles between oil changes. Self-adjusting brakes with bonded linings. Now just maybe you can beat a Chevy II's purchase price by a hair. But then, you're right back to driving plain.

CHEVROLET **Chevy II** GM
MARK OF EXCELLENCE
The stylish economy car

1967
Chevy II

It was in the 1967 model year that the Chevy II finally accomplished the task for which it had been created: outsell the Ford Falcon. That wasn't as great as it sounds. Combined production of Chevy II 100, Nova (opposite), and Nova SS models declined to approximately 106,500 for '67, a new low point for Chevrolet's conventional compact. Meanwhile, the Falcon had been suffering slipping demand, some of its sales drained off by the Mustang. Then a strike against Ford restricted assemblies to just 64,355 for the year. Though hard to believe by looking at them, the 1967 Chevy II was essentially the same car as the '62 under the skin. All-new sheetmetal was trotted out for 1966. A revised grille and energy-absorbing steering column were '67 additions.

The Oh-My-Heavens one. You release a few latches and those panels in the roof are ready for lift off. You release a few more and the rear window's ready for lift off. You flip the key in the ignition and you . . . and you . . . say, you're not listening. Hello, do you read us? What's the use. You're in a world all your own. **Corvette** Like a car, only better. CHEVROLET

10 seconds to lift off.

Sports Class winner of the *Motor Trend* 1968 Achievement Award, for which we thank them.

GM
MARK OF EXCELLENCE

1968
Corvette

What would prove to be the longest-running generation of Chevrolet's two-seat sports car made its debut in 1968. That's a bit ironic, given the criticisms the '68 stirred in the motoring press about things like styling, ride, passenger comfort and ergonomics, and build quality. There was no debate about the Corvette being powerful. Engines from a 300-hp 327 to a triple-carb 435-hp 427 were retained from 1967. Three- and four-speed manual transmissions were available, as was the Turbo Hydra-Matic automatic, which replaced the Powerglide. The chassis was similar to that of the 1963–67 cars, but front and rear tracks were widened. Styling flowed from the '65 Mako Shark II show car. Coupes came with removable roof panels, but soft tops still outsold them—for the last time.

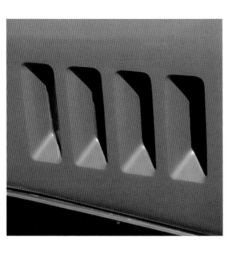

Chevelle SS 396 Sport Coupe. There's a convertible, too.

Its vigor remains undiluted by its comforts. (Another reason Chevelle's the most popular car in its field.)

Turbo-Jet 396 V8 (325 hp!) is standard on SS 396, not something you pay more for. An extra "charge" at no extra charge.

Special suspension and red-stripe wide-oval tires put more footprint on the road and hold it there firmly. SS 396 standard items.

4-speed shift is just what you ordered: big and hefty to handle all that torque; smooth shifting with a short, sure throw.

Bucket seats you specify, and you should. They're thickly cushioned, vinyl upholstered, comfortable as you can get and sporty looking, besides.

Four-Season Air Conditioning cools or warms as called for, dehumidifies and circulates air as you please. Weather's always good, when you order your own.

Stereo: available as FM multiplex radio (with AM, too) and/or 8-track tape player. Four speakers surround you with sound — pop, Bach or rock.

Quick-sized nimbleness, big-car ride, roominess, good looks: no wonder Chevelle sells so well. See your Chevrolet dealer and try a Chevelle for size.

SS 396

Chevelle **CHEVROLET**

Be smart. Be sure. Buy now at your Chevrolet dealer's.

1968
Chevelle

Chevrolet completely redid its market-leading intermediates for 1968, and right on time, too. Ford, Chrysler, and Chevy's GM stablemates did likewise with their midsize cars. The result? Chevelle came out on top again with a new high of 428,099 produced for the model year. The 115-inch wheelbase found under previous Chevelles was supplanted by a 112-inch stretch for all two-door cars and a 116-inch span with four-door models. Common styling details included a sloped deck with wraparound taillights and a crisp hood edge that formed a line that continued down the fenders and lower body. The SS 396 (right) returned as a $2899 hardtop coupe and $3102 convertible. They won 62,785 buyers drawn to the standard big-block power, beefier suspension, and all-vinyl interior.

Chevelle SS

Impala SS

Nova SS

Camaro SS

Chevrolet Sports Dept.

We'll bet you didn't know that nobody makes as many different kinds of sports models as Chevrolet does.

What's nice about this is that you can come to just one place, Chevrolet's Sports Department, and sample anything from a family-size Impala to a couple-size Corvette.

And, as you can see, we don't reserve the performance and handling glories for coupes alone. Chevrolet convertibles can also be outfitted with engines up to 427 cubic inches, tach and 4-speed, taut suspension and domed hood. With complete Super Sport equipment.

To put together one good performance model is no trick. But to build as many different kinds as you see here—ah, now that's our department. Main floor, at your Chevrolet dealer's.

CHEVROLET Be smart. Be sure. Buy now at your Chevrolet dealer's.

1968
Impala SS

The meteoric rise in popularity of intermediate muscle cars quickly left their full-sized fore-bears in the shade. By the late '60s, big-body sportsters clearly were down. They weren't quite out yet, though. After having been a true series from 1964 through '67, the Impala SS reverted to being an option package for 1968. The 36,432 owners of V8-equipped Impala convertibles, sport coupe hardtops, and new Custom hardtops (with the Caprice's formal roof) who shelled out $179.05 for option Z03 got vinyl bucket seats detailed in a distinctive pattern, a center console, wheel covers, and SS identification inside and out. (For serious perfor-mance, the SS 427 option would still be avail-able through '69.) Optional slotted rally wheels helped any Impala SS to better look the part.

'69 Kingswood Estate 3-Seat Walk-In Wagon.

Chevrolet introduces the walk-in wagon.

Here's a wagon that welcomes you in the back door without making you stoop over to keep from banging your head.

Now you simply walk up a step in the bumper and walk down a step inside. Then you simply turn around and sit right down.

Don't worry. We've slanted the back end to help keep the roof out of your way.

Another thoughtful design is our dual-action tailgate. Its concealed door-openers won't catch a sleeve like an outside handle.

Still another: Tri-Level loading in most wagons. Order a roof rack for load space on top, in addition to the load space you have inside and under the rear floor.

Performance? One quick answer is the new 327-cubic-inch V8, standard in many models. It's the largest standard V8 in its field.

Look over both our wagon sizes, biggest and big. Even the names are new. All at your Chevrolet dealer's now.

Just walk in.

CHEVROLET

Putting you first, keeps us first.

1969
Kingswood Estate

If you can't always beat 'em, sometimes it's wise to join 'em: That's essentially the story behind the "dual-action" tailgate that was a new feature for 1969 Chevrolet station wagons. In 1966, Ford introduced the "Magic Doorgate" with hinges at the bottom and the side that allowed tailgates to be lowered in the normal fashion to load cargo or opened at the side to ease passenger access. General Motors copied the undeniably convenient and flexible feature for '69 but cut a step into the rear bumper. Chevy's full-size wagon family was led by the Kingswood Estate with body woodgraining and a Caprice-like interior. The $3866 nine-passenger model had a rear-facing third seat. With rear seats down, it could hold 93 cubic feet of cargo—plus a bit more in an underfloor locker.

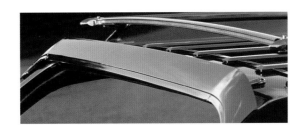

insert foot...

open mouth

Camaro SS Sport Coupe with Rally Sport equipment and Super Scoop hood.

Camaro's new Super Scoop.
Step on the gas and it steps up performance.

We really put our foot in it this time. Brought out a new Super Scoop hood you can order for Camaro SS and Z/28. It opens on acceleration and socks cool air to the carburetor for more power.

Camaro's got a lot of other scoops, too. It hugs the road with the widest tread of

any sportster at its price.

It's the only sportster with computer-selected springs.

Bucket seats, Astro Ventilation, full door-glass styling and wall-to-wall carpets are all standard equipment.

With the SS version, you get all this

plus a big V8, wide oval tires, power disc brakes and a special 3-speed with floor shift.

Your Chevrolet dealer's got the whole story on how the Hugger scoops the competition. Stop in. See for yourself. And step on it.

CHEVROLET

Putting you first, keeps us first.

1969

Camaro

Chevy's Mustang-fighter had a long and busy year in 1969. The first-generation Camaro wrapped up its three-year run with a thorough facelift, introduced some new features, paced the Indianapolis 500, and captured the Sports Car Club of America Trans-Am series championship. Thanks to a long build-out to cover the delayed introduction of the all-new 1970 model, production was a record 243,015 cars. Speed streaks off the wheel openings and a deeply vee'd grille—on cars without the hidden-head-lamp Rally Sport option—highlighted the revised looks. The Camaro SS and Z-28 (right) could be ordered with the new $79 Super Scoop hood that sucked in air at the cowl from the high-pressure area just ahead of the windshield when a determined driver put his foot down.

Chevelles appeal to two age groups. Under 30. And over.

SS 396 Sport Coupe

One reason Chevelles move so many different people is that there are so many different Chevelles to move.

You could buy a Garnet Red SS 396 Sport Coupe with domed hood, sport wheels, beefed-up suspension and a whole lot more.

Or a nice Tuxedo Black 300 Deluxe Sedan with a frugal 140-hp Six and few if any extras.

Chevelles are different all right. From each other. And from other cars.

No other mid-size car handles quite this nimble, or looks (in our humble opinion) quite this great.

No other mid-size car has an anti-theft locking system, computer-selected springs, inner fenders, and an acrylic lacquer finish. At least not at our price.

Chevelle, the most popular mid-size car.

The one with friends on both sides of the generation gap.

CHEVROLET

Putting you first, keeps us first.

See Olympic Gold Medalist Jean-Claude Killy, weekly, CBS-TV. Check your local TV listings.

1969
Chevelle

A little bit of cosmetic surgery and a few equipment substitutions were all it took to turn the 1969 Chevelle into a car that more than half a million motorists wanted to own, the vast majority of them flocking to the Malibu (opposite). Up front was a tidier new grille treatment. A taller taillight/back-up light ensemble freshened the rear. Malibus tacked on more lower-bodyside trim; SS 396s wore less. The flow-through "Astro Ventilation" system allowed convertibles and two-door hardtops to abandon side-window ventwings, following the lead some other Chevys had shown in '68. A pair of 350-cid V8s replaced 327s on the options list. The SS was turned into an option group for any two-door Chevelle, meaning that even the low-cost 300 Deluxe pillared coupe could flex some muscle.

With this one beautiful exception, there is no such thing as a true American sports car.

'69 Corvette CHEVROLET

1969
Corvette Stingray

Though its basic package was just a year old, the 1969 Corvette did not rest on its laurels. Several changes added up to make it better than the '68 car. Looks went virtually untouched other than to move the back-up lights into the inboard taillight lenses from a spot below the bumpers—and to restore the Stingray name-plate (now one word) to the front fenders. Altered interior door panels and a smaller-diameter steering wheel opened up a bit more space. The frame was stiffened and standard wheels were wider. A 350-cid V8 in 300- and 350-hp ratings was the new small-block engine. A 430-hp aluminum-head L88 427 (opposite) was still available and two cars came from the factory with all-aluminum ZL1 big-blocks. Production hit 38,762, a record that would stand until 1976.

Chevrolet put it all together.
Solid gentlemanly comfort without bombast. Sailplane silence.
Computer-selected coil springs for a ride that glides.
Yet Monte Carlo's handling leaves you feeling like anything but a fifth wheel. A taut 116″ wheelbase and a track five feet wide go where pointed. Precisely.
And powerfully: a 350-cubic-inch V8 is basic. (Order on up to a 454.)
Standard is an instrument panel with the rare look of hand-rubbed burled elm.
And Astro Ventilation.
Even power disc brakes, fiberglass-belted tires and higher intensity headlights.

It's all there.
At a Chevrolet price.
Monte Carlo.
The only car in its field. Period.

Putting you first, keeps us first. **On The Move.**

A group picture of all the cars in Monte Carlo's field.

1970
Monte Carlo

If there was one product niche that Chevrolet had avoided contesting with Ford, it was the "personal-luxury" segment that had been created by the Thunderbird. That all changed in 1970 with the introduction of the Monte Carlo. A slick bit of repackaging, the formally styled V8-only two-door hardtop was designed to fit over the 116-inch-wheelbase four-door Chevelle chassis. It quickly became famous for two things: having the longest hood in Chevy history and being the division's first spinoff car with a name that *didn't* begin with a C. At $3123 to start, it undercut the cheapest '70 T-Bird by $1800, and the 130,657 made swamped the production total of its established rival. That number included 3823 with the SS option (opposite) that featured a new 360-hp 454-cid V8 and chassis enhancements.

1970
Camaro Z28

Considering that they had to use some Chevy II underbody components that preset certain dimensions for the original Camaro, not every designer was happy with the outcome. The 1970 second-generation car put smiles on more faces in the styling studio. Its low, wide look with pronounced headlight pods, prominent rectangular grille, and sloped roofline (the convertible was gone) virtually screamed sport. It captured headlines when it finally arrived in February '70 after being waylaid by development delays. An array of 6s and small- and big-block V8s were available in other Camaros, but the race-bred Z28 now came with a 360-hp 350 that made it capable of mid-14-second quarter-mile times. Stouter suspension parts, a decklid spoiler, and 15×7 wheels were also found on Z28s.

1970 Chevelle SS 396.

It's getting tougher and tougher to resist.

The standard V8 has been kicked up to 350 hp.

A new air-gulping Cowl Induction Hood awaits your order.

You can also order your choice of a floor-mounted 4-speed or the 3-range Turbo Hydra-matic.

Under that lean and hungry look is a lean and agile suspension. F70 x 14 white-lettered wide oval treads. 7"-wide mag-type wheels. And power disc brakes.

Your mission is to infiltrate your Chevy dealer's and escape with this car.

It will go willingly.

Putting you first, keeps us first.

 CHEVROLET

On the move.

In ten seconds, your resistance will self-destruct.

1970
Chevelle SS

In 1970, it was all about the horsepower. The ever-quickening V8-driven horsepower race being run since the early '50s crossed the finish line that year. With rising insurance rates for hot cars squeezing consumers and government clean-air regulations facing manufacturers, what was left of the muscle car era after '70 was just a cool-down lap by comparison. Chevrolet capped this golden age of go with a Chevelle SS powered by the most powerful engine it had yet produced, the 454-cid LS6. With an 11.25:1 compression ratio, it generated 450 hp at 5600 rpm and 500 pound-feet of torque at 3600 rpm—enough power to break 13.5 seconds in the quarter-mile. An LS5 454 made "only" 360 hp. A pair of 396s (displacement was actually up to 402 cubes) spun out 350 and 375 hp.

1971.
You've changed. We've changed.

For 1971, we bring you the biggest Chevrolet ever.

And we bring you the littlest Chevrolet ever.

Caprice. Totally changed. With more ride, more handling, more luxury and more security than you've ever known in a Chevrolet before.

Best of all, we still give you Caprice at a Chevrolet price.

And if the most inexpensive car ever built is out of range, we give you the most inexpensive Chevrolet.

Our new Vega.

It's the little economy car that does everything. And does it well.

You'll do well to see them both. At your Chevrolet dealer's now.

Chevrolet

1971
Full-Sized Cars

The largest Chevrolets ever built made their bow for the 1971 model year. Wheelbase grew for the first time since '59 to 121.5 inches (125 for station wagons). Coil springs were continued all around except on wagons, which used rear leaf springs. The top-line Caprice continued in two hardtop models. It now sported a grille distinct from the other big Chevys, aping the Cadillac eggcrate look. The runaway popularity leader was still the Impala (opposite) in five body styles, including a convertible. Budget four-door sedans were found in the Bel Air and Biscayne ranks. Wagons, which featured a retractable "Glide Away" tailgate, came in Kingswood Estate, Kingswood, Townsman, and Brookwood trim. Some models came with a standard 6 and three-speed stickshift, but most had V8s.

Your new Nova.

It keeps on rolling along.

Out on the Mississippi, time drifts back 100 years. To the days when sternwheelers like the Delta Queen linked the river ports of mid-America.

Once aboard, you become part of the unchanging life on the river.

America. There's so much to see.

And you could hardly find a more dependable way to see it than in the 1972 Chevy Nova.

Actually, this year's Nova is pretty much unchanged from last year's Nova. The car independent auto mechanics said was "easiest to service" and had the "least mechanical problems." (Compared to *all* cars, in a survey conducted by *Motor Service* and *Service Station Management* magazines.)

With a car as dependable and economical as Nova, you don't go redoing it from one year to the next.

Mechanical improvements, yes. Like modifications in the generator, and in the rear axle, to make them even more durable. And improved emission controls for cleaner air.

Let's just say we do what ought to be done.

Because we want your new Nova to be the best car you ever owned.

Take your family aboard the Nova for a trial run.

At your Chevy dealer's.

Chevrolet

Highway safety begins at home. Buckle up before you leave.

1972 Nova Coupe with the famous Delta Queen riverboat on the Mississippi.

Chevrolet. Building a better   way to see the U.S.A.

1972
Nova

As many at Chevrolet predicted when the division's front-engine, rear-drive compact was introduced, it would outlive the Corvair. In fact, the Nova (the Chevy II part of the name faded out by the end of the '60s) went on to deliver hardy service through 1979. The 1972 model was the last with the general appearance of the all-new Chevy II Nova that came to market for '68. Since then, only items like grilles, taillights, wheel covers, and a few interior details had changed. The 1968–72 cars came only as a coupe and four-door sedan on a 111-inch wheelbase. A 4-cylinder engine had been available until 1970, but the '72s had a 250-cube 6 and small-block V8s of 307 and 350 cid, all now rated in lower "real-world" net horsepower. An SS option featured the 350.

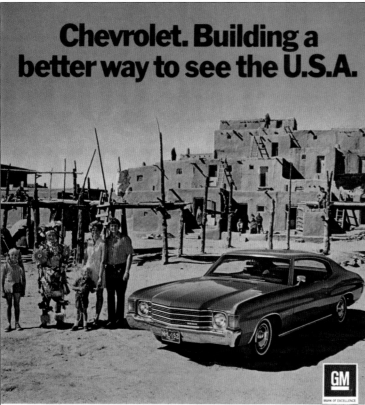

Chevelle Malibu Sport Coupe at the Taos Pueblo in Northern New Mexico.

1972
Chevelle Malibu

The Chevelle was supposed to deliver family car qualities in a tidier and more-economical form than the full-size standards. It seems, though, that Chevelle owners liked their style, too. The untouchable popularity leader of what was a very popular family of cars was the Malibu two-door hardtop, 212,388 of which were made, all but 4790 with a V8 engine. Number 2? It was the "sensible shoes" Malibu four-door sedan that drew 48,575 orders. Still, the Chevelle finally ceded the top spot in the midsize market to an all-new Ford Torino. Indeed, the intermediate Chevy was to have been completely redone, but a strike and other problems delayed a replacement. A grille divided horizontally into thirds and single-block parking lights differentiated the '72s from the previous year's Chevelle.

1972
Corvette Stingray

Even though the Mako Shark II-inspired design would last until 1982, the '72 Stingray marked the end of an era of sorts for the Corvette. It was the final one with chrome bumpers front and rear; federal bumper resilience standards would usher in a new front bumper under a body-color cover in '73. It was also the last of the '68-generation cars with a removable coupe rear window, pop-up cover panel for the windshield wipers, and 1970-vintage styling tweaks (flared wheel openings, rectangular parking lights, and eggcrate grille and fender-vent surfaces). Detuned engine offerings were restricted to a standard 350 V8 of 200 net hp, solid-lifter LT1 350 of 255 hp, and a 270-hp 454. The LT1 was in its final year. It could be ordered with a $1010 performance-oriented ZR1 option.

1973
Caprice Classic

In 1973, Chevrolet's luxury leader had its best year ever to that point. Orders for the Caprice Classic (the new name for the series) totaled 275,258 cars. That was still 43 percent of the number of more-popularly priced Impalas built, but the Caprice was gaining on its sibling and would, in fact, overtake it by the end of the '70s. The sales leader of the Caprice Classics was the stylish two-door hardtop (opposite) with its distinctive concave rear window. Production of the $4082 car came to 77,134 units. The rest of the six-model lineup included a convertible (newly shifted over from the Impala series), four-door hardtop, four-door sedan (added in '72), and two- and three-seat Estate wagons. Square taillights and government-spec front "crash" bumpers modified the looks of the '73s.

Laguna Colonnade Hardtop Coupe at the Rockwell Museum, Stockbridge, Mass.

Introducing Laguna. The new top-of-the-line Chevelle.

Good news, Chevelle people. You can move up to more car without leaving the make you love most.

Laguna is a new kind of Chevelle, the top of the line.

The distinctively styled front end is covered completely by resilient, protective urethane to resist dents.

Laguna has among other things a special body-color rear bumper.

Inside: special fabrics, special steering wheel and woodgrain accents.

Laguna, like all '73 Chevelles, has new front disc brakes, flow-through power ventilation, more glass area for improved visibility and more back seat leg room.

There's a power-operated moonroof you can add.

You're going to like the Laguna. A lot.

1973 Chevrolet. Building a better way to see the U.S.A. Chevrolet

1973
Chevelle

What was to have been the 1972 Chevelle finally appeared for '73. Presented in three series— Deluxe, Malibu, and new top-line Laguna—the new Chevy intermediates wore GM's "colonnade" styling theme. Built as coupes, four-door sedans, and four-door station wagons, they featured frameless door glass, but true pillarless hardtops and convertibles were a thing of the past. Two-door cars had fixed-position windows in their rear quarters. Wheelbases remained at 112 and 116 inches, but tread was widened and front disc brakes became standard. Most had base 250-cid 6 and 307-cid V8 engines, with a pair of 350 V8s and a 245-hp big-block 454 optional. (Lagunas started with a 350.) Other extras included swivel bucket seats in coupes and SS gear for Malibu coupes and wagons.

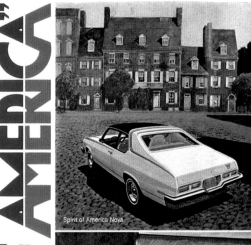

"SPIRIT OF AMERICA"

A limited edition of Chevrolets in America's favorite colors.

The colors are red, white and blue. The cars are Limited Edition Impalas, Novas and Vegas.

They're the special Spirit of America Chevrolets arriving at your Chevy dealer's right now.

They're cars known for their value. Distinctly styled with special interiors and equipment. Packaged like no Chevrolet before. Available for a limited time only.

Get the Spirit at your Chevy dealer's while they last.

The Spirit of America Impala package: • White or blue exterior. • Special white padded vinyl roof. • Special striping. • Special white wheels with paint stripes and trim rings. • Spirit of America crests. • Dual Sport mirrors, LH remote-control. • Wheel-opening moldings and fender skirts. • Bumper impact strips. • White all-vinyl interior trim with blue or red accents and carpeting. • Deluxe seat and shoulder belts. • Quiet Sound Group body insulation.

The Spirit of America Nova package: • White exterior. • Black touring-style vinyl roof. • Special striping. • Spirit of America decals. • White rally wheels with trim rings and special hubs. • Black dual Sport mirrors, LH remote-control. • Black grille. • E78-14 white-stripe tires. • White all-vinyl bucket seat interior. • Red carpeting.

The Spirit of America Vega package: • White exterior. • White vinyl roof. • Special striping. • Spirit of America decals. • White GT wheels with trim rings. • Custom Exterior. • Black-finished body sills. • White LH remote Sport mirror. • A70-13 white-lettered tires. • White all-vinyl Custom Interior. • Red carpeting.

Spirit of America Nova.

Spirit of America Vega.

Spirit of America Impala.

GM

1974
Vega

A press of increasing import sales in the late '60s convinced GM President Ed Cole that the division he once headed needed a cutting-edge subcompact to take on the world. Instead, he got the Vega. As maligned as the little car was during its 1971–77 lifetime, it's easy to forget that it was the product of some advanced—but unperfected—ideas in its engineering, manufacturing, and even its shipping. The 97-inch-wheelbase car arrived as a hatchback coupe, notchback coupe with conventional trunk, two-door station wagon, and sedan delivery. It was powered by an aluminum-block 140-cid overhead-camshaft 4 that ultimately proved troublesome. Sporty GT and plusher LX models were added over time. In 1974, Chevy put out a trio of patriotic "Spirit of America" models, including a Vega hatchback.